SALIENT DATES IN AMERICAN EDUCATION

Exploration Series in Education
Under the Advisory Editorship of
JOHN GUY FOWLKES

Salient Dates
in
American Education:
1635-1964

★ ★ ★ ★ ★

EDWARD A. KRUG

School of Education, University of Wisconsin

Harper & Row, Publishers, New York

Contents

v

Editor's Introduction

MORE THAN EVER BEFORE, programs for educational opportunity are discussed, not only in the U.S. but throughout the world. In daily newspapers; weekly, monthly and quarterly magazines; and books, both hardcover and paperback, existing educational programs are evaluated and recommendations for correction and modification are offered.

The National Defense Education Act of 1958 and the 1964 amendments to that act, together with the Economic Opportunity Act of 1964, and the Elementary and Secondary Education Act of 1965 have sweeping implications for the development of educational programs in the U.S.

These evidences of public and governmental interest in education are indeed heartening, not only to those professionally occupied in the field of education, but, indeed, to every citizen of the U.S. The development of interest and legislation also imposes an obligation upon every citizen to become as familiar as possible with educational needs and corresponding programs.

It seemed to me that familiarity with the critical events in the development of American education might prove helpful in the formulation of sound judgments of educational needs and programs. I encouraged E. A. Krug to write the work presented here—a concise chronicle of critical points in American education.

The thirty-five *Salient Dates in American Education* chosen by Krug include items of state and federal legislation, matters presented by private organizations, Supreme Court decisions, proposals by individuals, and actions of local communities.

It will be observed that out of the 359-year period described by Krug, eleven of the thirty-five *Salient Dates* occur in the twentieth century. It seems likely that we shall see in the remaining years of this century numerous proposals, actions, and legislation concerned with improved educational opportunity. This volume should prove to be of interest and value not only to those particularly concerned with education, but to all who desire to gain a wider and deeper understanding of the background of American education.

JOHN GUY FOWLKES

May, 1965

Preface

THIS IS AN ANNOTATED CALENDAR OF EVENTS in the history of American education. Military history has its campaigns and battles, political history its presidents, prime ministers, and kings. History other than military and political often lacks such frameworks. It is the purpose of this book to supply one for a phase of social history.

The events presented here cover a broad range of topics, including elementary, secondary, and higher education; vocational education; public and private schools; state and local school systems; teacher education; and the role of the federal government in education. Included also are people, such as Thomas Jefferson, Benjamin Franklin, Horace Mann, William Holmes McGuffey, Charles W. Eliot, and Clarence Kingsley.

I have found this framework useful in the teaching of a course called "School and Society" at the University of Wisconsin. It may be useful in a variety of courses in education and in American history, as well as of interest to the general public.

E. A. K.

SALIENT DATES IN AMERICAN EDUCATION

★ ★ ★ ★ ★ ★ 1635 ★ ★ ★ ★ ★ ★

The Boston Public Latin School

A PUBLIC MEETING took place in Boston on April 13, 1635. Those who were present entreated Brother Philemon Pormort, otherwise little known in history, to serve as schoolmaster for the teaching and nurturing of their children. In so doing, they fixed this date as the beginning of school history in New England. No record was left of Pormort's reply to the meeting, and the school itself probably was not started until the following year.

Presumably this was a grammar school, meaning the grammar of Latin. In any case, the present Public Latin School of Boston traces its ancestry back to this meeting of 1635. Other communities in Massachusetts Bay Colony, as well as some in Plymouth and in Connecticut, soon followed the example set in the Boston meeting. By 1700 there were 26 schools of Latin grammar in the New England colonies, clearly identified as such.

The model for these schools came from old England, where there had been at least 300 such in 1600, three decades before the founding of Boston. Grammar schools in England often taught both Latin and Greek. Although preparing some of their pupils for Oxford and Cambridge, they taught many who went no farther than the grammar-school course. Greek was perhaps a polite accomplishment, but Latin was necessary, or at least useful, in a variety of

1

occupations. The course was usually seven years long, and those who completed it allegedly could use Latin as a living tongue. What they learned of other subjects came through the books they read in the classics. History, natural science, and even mathematics were not studied as such.

Grammar schools in New England followed much the same curriculum. Some of them, however, did teach reading and writing in English, perhaps with a little ciphering, and it was not until 1699 that the school in Boston was officially called the Latin School. The earliest document corresponding to a course of study was written by Nathaniel Williams of the Boston school in 1712. In the seven-year program there outlined, the pupils read Erasmus, Cicero, Ovid, Horace, and other authors in Latin, along with the New Testament, Isocrates, Homer, and Hesiod in Greek.

There is always the temptation to regard these as secondary schools, but the idea of secondary education, even the term itself, probably did not appear until the nineteenth century. The pupils of these grammar schools were not adolescents, at least not until they were nearly through the course. Boys (for these were strictly all-male establishments) entered these schools usually at eight and finished at fifteen. Before entering, they had presumably learned the rudiments of reading in English, either at home or in a reading school. Some of those who finished went to Harvard. In this way the grammar schools were what some would later call middle schools and indirectly the ancestors of schools referred to as secondary.

The Boston Latin School is called the oldest public school in North America; correspondingly, the meeting of April 13, 1635, is hailed as the beginning of the American public school system. Distinctions between public and private schools, however, emerged only gradually in American school history. According to the town clerk of Boston in 1636, the funds for the school came as donations from the richer inhabitants. Income was later provided from the rental of town lands and from the town tax. The school was freely open to boys of all classes. Only nonresidents paid tuition; both they and the town dwellers sometimes paid special admission fees and charges for fuel. Town meetings appointed the masters and fixed the locations of the schools. In the light of these practices, the Boston school was clearly what would later be considered a public school, and it has so remained, being now a part of the Boston public school system.

Relatively few boys in New England attended these grammar schools. The combined enrollments of the Boston Latin School and its North Boston counterpart (1713–1789) reached 202 students in 1769, which was the high point shown in the records kept between 1738 and 1789. The extent to which wealth and social class affected attendance is not known, but may be surmised. Poor families could ill afford to take a boy out of economic production for seven years, but not even well-to-do families necessarily felt it was worth the effort. The desire of a family to provide this kind of education was probably the deciding point. While attendance at a grammar school was helpful in preparing for college, it was not required; many boys got this preparation through tutoring or through studying by themselves.

Most of the grammar schools of New England were absorbed by or joined other kinds of schools during the first part of the nineteenth century. The Boston school, however, gathered strength and momentum with the passing of time, its enrollments going over the 2,000 mark in the late 1920s. It has changed its location several times and has on occasion modified its program. The course of study has varied from four to eight years; in the present century the main program has consisted of a six-year course.

Arithmetic was added to the course of study in 1814 and the elements of geometry and algebra five years later. Modern academic subjects, such as history, French, German, and the sciences came in, but the classics remained. In one respect the school has continued adamant, still admitting boys only. Mindful of this omission, the city fathers of Boston in 1878 opened a separate classical high school for girls.

Suggestions for Additional Reading

Holmes, Pauline. *A Tercentenary History of the Boston Public Latin School 1635–1935.* Cambridge, Massachusetts: Harvard University Press, 1935.

Marson, Philip. *Breeder of Democracy.* Cambridge, Massachusetts: Schenkman Publishing Company, Inc., 1963. A history and interpretation of the Boston Public Latin School by a member of its faculty.

Morison, Samuel Eliot. *The Intellectual Life of Colonial New England.* Ithaca, N.Y.: Cornell University Press Great Seal Books, 1961. Chap. IV.

Harvard College

On October 28, 1636, the General Court of Massachusetts Bay Colony voted 400 pounds of public funds for a school or college. A year later the succeeding court ordered that the college be located at Newtown, just across the Charles River from Boston, with twelve leading men of the colony named to get the college started. By the summer of 1638, the name of Newtown had been changed to Cambridge, and the college was ready for business with students (male only), a building, and a professor.

At this point the college still had no name. On September 14, 1638, John Harvard, a newly-arrived clergyman from England, died, leaving to the college a bequest of 779 pounds, 17 shillings, and 2 pence, plus a library of several hundred books. As the money came to twice the amount originally voted from the public funds, this was no small bequest. In appropriate recognition thereof, the General Court, in March of the following year, ordered that the college be named Harvard.

Whether John Harvard would have been happy with his college during its infant year is another matter. The first professor, or master, Nathaniel Eaton, was a bad choice, lacking apparently the moral character and sweetness of temper often claimed as the fruits of a classical education. He was removed from his post in September, 1639 after a scandalous episode involving his beating of an assistant teacher. The college was closed and not reopened until the following year, this time with Henry Dunster as professor.

Things went better under Dunster, and the year 1642 witnessed the appearance of Harvard's first graduating class, consisting of nine students. A favorable report on the college appeared in *New England's First Fruits,* written in New England but published in London in 1643. This document contained much praise of Dunster and of the master of the Cambridge Grammar School, the latter being commended for "his abilities, dexterity, and painfulness in teaching."[1] It also presented the rules and precepts of the college, along with the requirements for admission and the program of studies.

"When any scholar is able to understand Tully [Cicero]," stated *New England's First Fruits,* "or such like classical Latin author extempore, and make and speak true Latin in verse and prose, *suo ut aiunt Marte;* and decline perfectly the paradigms of nouns and verbs in the Greek tongue: Let him then and not before be capable of admission into the college."

Once admitted, the scholar began a three-year course that included logic, ethics, and politics; arithmetic, geometry, astronomy, physics, and "the nature of plants"; Hebrew and "the Eastern tongues"; some history; and more Greek. Dunster and other leaders of the Massachusetts Bay Colony had attended Cambridge University in England, and this program was modeled on the Arts Course of that institution.

With some modifications, this set the pattern for American colleges of liberal arts. Harvard also defined the college ideal that sought to take broadly into account the lives and characters of the students. The rules and precepts directed the students toward diligent and studious deportment and warned them against the society of men who led unfit and dissolute lives. As each of the separate colleges at Oxford and Cambridge constituted a center of fellowship for its students, so did Harvard provide not just a course of study, but a residential community dedicated to the intellectual and moral life.

[1] *New England's First Fruits.* For books in which this document is reproduced see Suggestions for Additional Reading.

Those who seek a sharp line of distinction between public and private education have found Harvard a curious case indeed. At the outset it was clearly a public institution in the most modern sense. It was founded by the legislative body of the colony and received its first money from that source. Like other public colleges and universities that followed, it did not refuse bequests from private donors, such as the substantial one from John Harvard. It continued to draw public funds until 1824. The Board of Overseers, established by the General Court in 1642, consisted of the governor, the deputy governor, and the magistrates of the colony, plus the teaching elders from the churches of the six adjoining towns and the professor (president) of the college.

As time passed, the public image was modified and the private character of Harvard began to emerge. In a charter granted in 1650 by the General Court, direct administration was vested in a self-perpetuating corporation called the Presidents and Fellows of Harvard College to act under the general supervision of the overseers. This charter was confirmed by Massachusetts in its constitution of 1780. During the nineteenth century changes took place in the manner of naming the overseers; an act of 1851 turned this over to the legislature. In 1856, however, the election of the overseers was assigned to the graduates of the college. This removed the last direct control by the state.

Harvard was not the first institution of higher learning in the New World. Both the Royal University of Mexico and the University of San Marcos in Lima had been founded in 1551, nearly a century before. Neither of these institutions, however, was in a position to transmit the heritage of ancient and medieval learning to the English colonies far to the north. The initial vehicle for this continuity into our society was clearly provided by the General Court of Massachusetts Bay Colony in its action of 1636. As set forth in the text of *New England's First Fruits* and proclaimed on the Harvard gate today, what the colonists wanted after establishing their government and building their churches was "to advance learning and perpetuate it to posterity."

Suggestions for Additional Reading

Morison, Samuel Eliot. *The Founding of Harvard College*. Cambridge, Massachusetts: Harvard University Press, 1935. Contains the text of *New England's First Fruits,* Appendix D, pp. 420–446.

Hofstadter, Richard, and Wilson Smith. *American Higher Education: A Documentary History*. 2 vols. Chicago: The University of Chicago Press, 1961. Contains part of *New England's First Fruits* and other documents pertaining to the early history of Harvard, Vol. I, pp. 5–32.

Old Deluder Law
of Massachusetts Bay Colony

BY THE YEAR 1647, the Colony of Massachusetts Bay had nearly 20,000 people, some 30 towns, 30 to 40 churches, 7 grammar schools, and a college. Five years before, the General Court in its law of 1642 had taken note of what would later be called elementary education, directing the selectmen of the towns to see that parents and masters taught the children in their care to read the English tongue. The law of 1642 said nothing about schools, although some vernacular schools for young children probably existed at the time.

Evidently not satisfied with this, the General Court in its law of November 11, 1647, ordered the towns to supply teachers as well. This was the famous Old Deluder Law, in which the need for the action taken is charged to Satan himself. Whether or not Satan had been deluding the children of Massachusetts, it is the contention of some writers that the law of 1647 deluded whole generations of historians.

In any case, the text of the law is well worth examination:

It being one chief project of the old deluder, Satan, to keep men from the knowledge of the Scriptures, as in former times by keeping them in an unknown tongue, so in these latter times by persuading them from the use of tongues that so at least the true sense and

9

meaning of the original might be clouded by false glosses of saint-seeming deceivers, that learning may not be buried in the grave of our fathers in the church and commonwealth, the Lord assisting our endeavors,

It is therefore ordered, that every township in this jurisdiction, after the Lord hath increased them to the number of fifty householders, shall then forthwith appoint one within their town to teach all such children as shall resort to him to write and read, whose wages shall be paid either by the parents or masters of such children, or by the inhabitants in general, by way of supply, as the major part of those that order the prudentials of the town shall appoint; provided, those that send their children be not oppressed by paying much more than they can have them taught for in other towns; and it is further ordered, that where any town shall increase to the number of one hundred families or householders they shall set up a grammar school, the master thereof being able to instruct youth so far as they may be fitted for the university; provided, that if any town neglect the performance hereof above one year, that every such town shall pay five pounds to the next school till they shall perform this order."[1]

The reference to Bible reading as protection against Satanic projects has suggested a strong religious motive for this law, and it raises the larger question of the degree to which school legislation in New England involved religious rather than secular considerations. It has long been taken for granted that such was the case. This view, however, has been challenged by Shipton and by Morison,[2] the latter being inclined to the opinion that the religious note was included to make the law more acceptable. Other pedagogical statements in Massachusetts Bay Colony usually added the secular aims. The law of 1642 had called for the rearing of children in some honest calling or employment. Harvard's charter of

---

[1] Massachusetts Bay law of November 11, 1647.

[2] Clifford K. Shipton, "Secondary Education in the Puritan Colonies," *The New England Quarterly*, VII (December, 1934), 646–661; Samuel Eliot Morison, *The Intellectual Life of Colonial New England* (Ithaca, N.Y.: Cornell University Press Great Seal Books, 1961), pp. 65–69.

1650 identified the advancement of literature, sciences, and the arts as the reason why people gave lands and money to the college.

These speculations do not resolve the question of why the colony took a step of this kind, one not without precedent, since both Scotland and the Netherlands had made similar provisions, but one without precedent in the English society from which the settlers of Massachusetts had come. Neither do they account for the strong drive toward state-directed education that persisted in the New England setting and later spread to other parts of the country. According to Bailyn,[3] the educational provisions of family, community, and church as known in England tended to break down in the wilderness environment of the New World. School legislation, therefore, appeared. Many proponents of particular kinds of schooling, of course, have argued for their causes, such as manual training, on the grounds that such functions were no longer being taken care of in the home.

Other controversial matters growing out of the law of 1647 involve the degree to which it was enforced and the quality of the schools themselves. According to one point of view, the people of Massachusetts Bay overthrew ecclesiastical domination at the end of the seventeenth century and then let their schools decline. The eighteenth century has been portrayed as a long period of deterioration in schools. Against this, Shipton has argued that the eighteenth century was an era of improvement in the public school system.[4] In any case, many people in New England learned to read and to write. Also involved is the question of education for girls. The law of 1647 assigned to the vernacular schoolmaster "all such children as shall resort to him"; on the other hand, grammar schools were for boys only. Even on this point, Shipton contends that private and informal provisions did exist for the education of girls in the classical tongues.[5]

---

[3] Bernard Bailyn, *Education in the Forming of American Society* (Chapel Hill, N.C.: The University of North Carolina Press, 1960), pp. 15–29.

[4] Shipton, *op. cit.*, p. 655.

[5] *Ibid.*, p. 659.

One thing that the law of 1647 did not compel was school attendance. This was to wait for the passing of two more centuries. The law required the towns to provide teachers, but did not say that anyone had to resort to them. Neither did the law clearly require the towns to provide free schools, although it stipulated that the local inhabitants not have to pay "much more" than the price for which they could buy schooling in other towns.

The function assigned by the law of 1647 to the grammar schools was that of preparation for "the university." Earlier, *New England's First Fruits* had stated a similar function for the Cambridge Grammar School. Morison, however, has made the guess that less than half the graduates of the grammar schools went to the college in the period before 1690.[6] Perhaps this provision of the law of 1647 is the seed of the widespread modern notion that some fields of study are appropriate only for college-bound students.

Suggestions for Additional Reading

Bailyn, Bernard. *Education in the Forming of American Society.* Chapel Hill, N.C.: The University of North Carolina Press, 1960.

Commager, Henry Steele (ed.). *Documents of American History.* 6th ed. revised. New York: Appleton-Century-Crofts, Inc., 1958. Contains the law of 1642 and the law of 1647, pp. 28–29.

Cubberley, Ellwood P. (ed.). *Readings in Public Education in the United States.* Boston: Houghton Mifflin Company, 1934. Contains the law of 1642 and the law of 1647, plus other early school documents of New England, pp. 14–20.

Morison, Samuel Eliot. *The Intellectual Life of Colonial New England.* Ithaca, N.Y.: Great Seal Books, Cornell University Press, 1961. Chap. III.

[6] Morison, *op. cit.,* p. 90.

Franklin's Proposal for the Philadelphia Academy

"IT IS PROPOSED," wrote Benjamin Franklin in 1749, "that some persons of leisure and public spirit, apply for a charter, by which they may be incorporated, with power to erect an academy for the education of youth, to govern the same, provide masters, make rules, receive donations, purchase lands, etc. and to add to their number, from time to time such other persons as they shall judge suitable."[1]

With this as the key sentence in his *Proposals Relating to the Education of Youth in Pennsylvania,* Franklin went on to specify a program of studies. Conceding that the students should be taught all things useful and ornamental, he was willing to settle, since "art is long, and their time is short," for what would be most so. Among the studies he included were arithmetic, accounts, geometry, astronomy, the English language, modern languages, the classics, history, gardening, and good breeding. Some of these were to be optional with the students. Not every one, for example, would be compelled to study Latin and Greek, but "none that have an ardent desire to learn them should be refused; their English, arithmetic, and other studies absolutely necessary, being at the same time not neglected."

Franklin was a persuasive writer and a man of action. By the

[1] Benjamin Franklin, *Proposals Relating to the Education of Youth in Pennsylvania* (Philadelphia, 1749).

13

end of the following year he had assembled twenty-four trustees, including himself, and had collected both private and public funds. His academy was opened in Philadelphia on January 7, 1751; the announcement stated a curriculum similar to what Franklin had proposed, stipulating at the same time an entrance fee of 20 shillings and a tuition rate of 4 pounds a year. The charter for the school named it The Academy and Charitable School in the Province of Pennsylvania, the charitable school being an older institution taken over by the trustees.

Back of Franklin's proposals and his ability to carry them out extended a context including his own ideas, the development of some new kinds of schools in England, and the growth of industry and trade in American colonial life. In his home town of Boston, Franklin had briefly attended the Latin School, apparently without enthusiasm, for he came to express much skepticism about classical learning. His quick mind led him into a variety of philosophical, scientific, and historical pursuits. Among his many enterprises in Philadelphia, he started the Junto, called by him a club of mutual improvement, and the American Philosophical Society. These interests were consistent with his desire for pedagogical change, and he had started to promote the idea of an academy as far back as 1743.

He also had before him the example provided by academies in England, started by dissenters from the Anglican Church after the restoration of Charles II in 1660. The term *academy* went back to the grove in which Plato had conducted his school of higher studies. It was perhaps made attractive to dissenters by Milton's use of it in his treatise *Of Education,* written in 1644. Milton had suggested a broad program of modern studies along with Latin and Greek. No longer bound by the exclusively classical curricula of the grammar schools, the dissenting academies included English literature, modern languages, and modern history in their studies.

Meanwhile the American colonists had shown themselves to be inventive in spawning a variety of private-venture schools dedicated to modern and practical aims. One writer has identified fifty schools in Boston, New York, and Philadelphia between 1709 and 1758 that taught bookkeeping, navigation, or surveying, or combinations of these subjects.[2] Of these, twenty-seven were in existence before Franklin wrote his proposals in 1749. There were schools, including some of the above, that taught modern languages, mathematics, geography, and history. Many of these offered night classes.

Even the term *grammar school,* hitherto used only by schools that dedicated themselves to Latin and Greek, was taken over at least as early as 1732 by an institution in New York City that added to its Latin studies not only mathematics, but also geography, navigation, and bookkeeping. There was, then, much colonial precedent for the kind of school Franklin had in mind. Such schools as these, however, were business ventures conducted by relatively unknown entrepreneurs. Franklin's academy, while not a public school in the modern sense, was a broad community enterprise and one that has gained a wide historical press because of the name of its founder.

Once started, the academy in Philadelphia began rapidly changing its characteristics. It started in 1751 with two divisions, Latin and English, and was what would later be called a secondary school. Four years afterwards, the trustees, acting under a new charter, changed the name to the College and Academy of Philadelphia, with authority to grant degrees. A new plan in 1762 provided philosophy schools and Latin and Greek schools for the college part and an English school and a school of practical mathematics for the academy. In 1779, the state revoked the college charter. After a twelve-year period of confusion, the state in 1791 reorganized the enterprise as The Trustees of the University of Pennsylvania, consisting of the governor and a self-perpetuating board that chose its own successors. Thus it was that Franklin's academy ended as a university, one known today as a private institution, but testifying, like Harvard, to the difficulty of drawing the public-private distinction in times past.

In spite of his distinguished name, or perhaps because of the responsibilities attached to it, Franklin was unable to keep in close

[2] Robert Francis Seybolt, *Source Studies in American Colonial Education* (Urbana: The University of Illinois, 1925), pp. 108–109.

touch with the school he had created, and he disliked the way it went. His main interests lay in the modern studies; apparently he had included the classics in his proposal of 1749 only as a concession to the pedagogical opinions of the times. The trustees, he felt, fostered the classical studies and neglected the modern. In 1789, the year before his death, he expressed bitter complaint about this in a paper entitled *Observations Relative to the Intentions of the Original Founders of the Academy in Philadelphia.* Noting that with the fashion of curled and powdered hair a man could no longer wear his hat, known as a *chapeau bras,* on his head, but would carry it on his arm, Franklin sarcastically dismissed the study of Latin and Greek as the *chapeau bras* of modern literature.

It is difficult, therefore, to identify Franklin's academy in the line of what subsequently became the academy movement in American education. Standing as a somewhat isolated phenomenon, it is noteworthy none the less as the first community-wide attempt to break the classical monopoly in what would later be called secondary schools. Probably more significant than the school itself, Franklin's proposal of 1749 stands as an eloquent landmark in the polemical literature of pedagogy.

Suggestions for Additional Reading

Best, John Hardin (ed.). *Benjamin Franklin as Educator.* (Classics in Education No. 14.) New York: Bureau of Publications, Teachers College, Columbia University, 1962. Contains Franklin's 1749 *Proposals,* pp. 126–151, and other documents pertaining to the Philadelphia academy.

Franklin, Benjamin. *Proposals Relating to the Education of Youth in Pensilvania.* Facsimile reprint with introduction by William Pepper. Philadelphia: University of Pennsylvania Press, 1931.

Mulhern, James. *A History of Secondary Education in Pennsylvania.* Philadelphia: published by the author, 1933. Chap. VII.

The Phillips Academy, Andover, Massachusetts

THE IDENTIFIABLE BEGINNINGS of what became the American academy movement are found in the Phillips Academy of Andover, Massachusetts, founded on April 21, 1778. Chief mover in this enterprise was a young man named Samuel Phillips, Jr., whose father and uncle on that date executed the deed for its endowment. Probably little persuasion was needed, for the members of the Phillips family involved in this action, Harvard graduates all, were of one mind in their dedication to learning and virtue. Five years later, Uncle John on his own initiative opened the companion institution, the Phillips Academy of Exeter, New Hampshire, and contributed generously to its support as well.

Perhaps more directly than Franklin, young Phillips found his inspiration in the dissenting academies of England, particularly in the writings of Philip Doddridge, who conducted a famous school at Northampton. Like Franklin, Phillips was a man of practical interests; during 1776 he had experimented with techniques in the manufacture of gunpowder for the Continental army and later ran his own powder mill at Andover. It was while working on the gunpowder experiments with Eliphalet Pearson, later the first master of the Andover Academy, that he wrote of his desire for a school that would check the decay of virtue and the prevalence of vice.

Father Samuel and Uncle John Phillips endorsed these sentiments in their deed of gift, a document probably composed by Samuel Jr. himself. Contrasting the knowledge and virtue of which the mind was capable with "the prevalence of ignorance and vice, disorder and wickedness" in the world, they declared their purpose to be that of founding "a public free school or academy for the purpose of instructing youth, not only in English and Latin Grammar, Writing, Arithmetic, and those Sciences wherein they are commonly taught; but more especially to learn them the GREAT END AND REAL BUSINESS OF LIVING."[1]

What they meant by this great end and real business of living was clarified later in the document when they defined the "*first* and *principal* object" of the school to be "the promotion of true Piety and Virtue." To this they added three other aims: "the *second,* instruction in the English, Latin, and Greek languages, together with writing, arithmetic, music, and the art of speaking; the *third,* practical geometry, logic, and geography; and the *fourth,* such other of the liberal arts and sciences or languages as opportunity and ability may hereafter admit and as the Trustees shall direct."

Nine days after this document was executed, Master Eliphalet Pearson opened the school with thirteen boys. He reported to the trustees that he began school each day at eight o'clock with devotional exercises and the reading of a psalm, closing it at night with reflections, prayer, hymn singing, and readings from Dr. Doddridge's *Family Expositor.* Each scholar recited on Monday what he remembered from the sermons heard the previous day; on Saturday the bills were presented and punishments administered.

With the opening of the Exeter Academy in 1783, this one sponsored particularly by Uncle John, the twin institutions of the Phillips family were off on their long career in American education. The constitution of Exeter repeated the sentiments and virtually the same words as those in the Andover deed of gift. Like Franklin's academy at the time of its founding, these were private schools, but

---

[1] Deed of gift for the endowment of Phillips Andover Academy, April 21, 1779.

with public purpose. Unlike the Philadelphia venture, these schools did not become universities.

During the nineteenth century, both Andover and Exeter became identified to a marked degree with preparation for college and were referred to in a category known as the endowed preparatory schools. This was not the case in the early period, although their curricula did include Latin and Greek. Unlike the law of 1647 that specified preparation for college as the aim of the grammar schools, the documents of the Phillips academies stated no such aim. According to Williams this was a deliberate omission, one that probably reflected the specific convictions of Uncle John Phillips.[2]

It was undoubtedly the hope of the Phillips family that their venture would be imitated. Few hopes have been so amply fulfilled. By 1800 there were seventeen academies in Massachusetts, nineteen in New York, ten in Georgia, plus others scattered throughout various states. After 1800 the academy movement became a flood, with estimates of the number at midcentury coming to as high as six thousand.

The academies were spread throughout the land, from New England to the farthest frontiers. In the main they were what we would call private schools, but in some states they had complicated public relationships through incorporation and in some instances the receiving of funds. Although known by a wide variety of names, including seminaries, institutes, collegiate institutes, and colleges, they have as a group been identified with what we would call secondary education. Many of them, however, admitted very young children, and some of them competed openly with colleges, not only in name, but in fact. Most of their students did not go afterwards to colleges or universities.

There were day academies and boarding academies. Some were coeducational; others were maintained for boys or girls only. In general, the academy movement contributed mightily to the devel-

[2] Myron R. Williams, *The Story of Phillips Exeter* (Exeter, N.H.: The Phillips Exeter Academy, 1959), pp. 25–26.

opment of school opportunities for girls. They were established under a variety of auspices, including that of churches; many were private-venture establishments, depending heavily on fees.

Above all, academies were noted for the breadth and flexibility of their programs of study, these encompassing almost all the known sciences and arts. Requirements for admission were often negligible or nonexistent. Courses were shaped to the curiosity or interests of the students, and they anticipated much of what later came to be called individualized instruction. Inevitably, many of them were criticized for low standards and lack of scholarly ideals. Possibly the Phillips family would not have recognized or cared to own the vast progeny they had spawned. They would undoubtedly have approved of all academies that dedicated themselves to the cultivation of true piety and virtue.

Eventually most of the academies ceased to exist. By 1900 the old-time academy had faded into the folklore of a romantic American past. Surviving academies have become associated with wealth and social status, with preparation for college, and, in the minds of some, with scholastic standards higher than those of the public schools. This image of so-called elitism, however, is a comparatively recent phenomenon. Throughout much of the nineteenth century, the academies were the major vehicles of popular education beyond the common or district school.

Suggestions for Additional Reading

Sizer, Theodore R. (ed.). *The Age of the Academies.* (Classics in Education No. 22.) New York: Bureau of Publications, Teachers College, Columbia University, 1964. Contains the deed of gift of the Andover Academy, pp. 77–89.

Smith, J. W. Ashley. *The Birth of Modern Education: The Contribution of the Dissenting Academies 1660–1800.* London: Independent Press Ltd., 1954.

Williams, Myron R. *The Story of Phillips Exeter.* Exeter, N.H.: The Phillips Exeter Academy, 1957. Contains the deed of gift of the Exeter Academy, pp. 187–193.

Jefferson's Proposal for Free Schools in Virginia

THREE YEARS after the Declaration of Independence, Thomas Jefferson submitted a plan for a school system in Virginia, where he had just been elected governor. Although not enacted into law, this document of June, 1779, entitled *A Bill for the More General Diffusion of Knowledge,* was in itself a statement of much and enduring significance. It raised issues that are always pertinent and set forth what might be called the threads of Jeffersonianism in the fabric of American pedagogical thought.

Unlike the Massachusetts law of 1647, this bill reflected not the local emergence of institutions and practices, but rather a grand design, conceived in one man's lively imagination, complete with details on how the schools were to be organized and what subjects would be taught. Its aim was that of providing for the welfare of the political state, directed first of all at the enlightenment of a general electorate. Beyond this, it sought to furnish leaders "called to that charge without regard to wealth, birth or other accidental conditions or circumstances"[1] and duly educated for their responsibilities and tasks.

Beginning with the designation of small geographical units termed *hundreds,* Jefferson's bill directed the voters of each such area to select the location for their schoolhouse. The county alder-

[1] *A Bill for the More General Diffusion of Knowledge,* 1779.

men were to build the schools and appoint overseers, one for every ten of the hundreds, who in turn were to name the teachers and supervise their work.

Each local school was to teach reading, writing, and common arithmetic, with the reading books chosen to make the children "acquainted with Graecian, Roman, English, and American history." All the "free" boys and girls of the hundred were to receive their tuition "gratis" for three years. They could stay longer than three years on payment of fees.

Presumably the three years of free schooling were to provide a minimum degree of general enlightenment. The leaders, however, would not necessarily come from those who stayed longer in the local schools. These were to be drawn from students who would go from the local schools to residential grammar schools, some twenty in number throughout the state. Specified as fields of study in these grammar schools were "the Latin and Greek languages, English grammar, geography, and the higher part of numerical arithmetic, to wit, vulgar and decimal fractions, and the extraction of the square and cube roots."

These were to be tuition schools, but with subsidies for poor boys "of the best and most promising genius and disposition," one from every ten of the lower schools. All of these were to remain in the grammar schools for at least one year; two thirds would be selected for one year more. With the completion of the two-year course, one boy would be picked from each beginning group to attend the school four more years, or six in all. So long as a boy selected initially for these purposes remained at the grammar school, he was to receive free tuition, board, and lodging. Finally, half the group that finished the six-year course would be sent to William and Mary College, still with all expenses paid.

This would be a breathtaking proposal in any age. It would also be for many a most confusing one. Jefferson perplexed his contemporaries; he continues to perplex his modern readers as well. In his burning determination to exclude from educational opportunity any vestige of distinction based on wealth or social class, Jefferson would meet one criterion of practically all modern democratic thought. Yet he did not propose to make freely available a substantial amount of advanced education to more than a few. Jefferson believed in an aristocracy of intellectual talent, and on this he was far more selective than almost any modern advocate of rigorous standards in schools. On the other hand, although he called for systematic examination of all students by official visitors, he said nothing about excluding from the grammar schools on intellectual grounds those who could pay their way.

Jefferson cast some light on these enigmas two years later in his *Notes on the State of Virginia*. It had been his desire, he said, to furnish "to the wealthier part of the people convenient schools at which their children may be educated at their own expense." The general objects of his bill, however, had been "to provide an education adapted to the years, to the capacity, and the condition of every one, and directed to their freedom and happiness." Like others who find themselves trying to talk their way out of an uncomfortable position, he fell back on the excuse that "specific details" had not been appropriate for his earlier document.

With these general objects in view, Jefferson went on in his *Notes* to defend the elaborate selection of poor boys who could meet the highest intellectual standards. "By this means," he argued, "twenty of the best geniuses will be raked from the rubbish annually, and be instructed, at the public expense, so far as the grammar schools."[2] He suggested also that students not chosen for the final period of study at William and Mary might well become the future teachers in the grammar schools themselves. Those going on to the college were destined for some loftier role in the state! In any case, he made clear at this point his great fear that geniuses, whether at the first level for statecraft or at the second level for teaching in grammar schools, might be overlooked.

Although his *Bill for the More General Diffusion of Knowledge* failed to gain legislative approval, a subsequent General Assembly, meeting in 1796, did pass some of its features dealing with the pri-

[2] *Notes on the State of Virginia,* Query XIV, 1781.

mary schools. Unfortunately for the advocates of free schooling, the 1796 act required the court of each county to determine the year in which the Aldermen should be appointed for the purpose of setting the machinery in motion. No such years were ever determined by the courts, and no schools were established under this act.

Jefferson waited two more decades and then made his last major effort on behalf of a state system of free schools. In his *Bill for Establishing a System of Public Education,* submitted to the General Assembly in 1817, he included, with some changes in terminology and procedure, most of the provisions from his bill of 1779, adding to these his plan for the University of Virginia. The general bill languished in the Assembly, with Jefferson complaining to his friend George Ticknor on November 25, 1817, that the members did not "generally possess information enough to perceive the important truths, that knowledge is power, that knowledge is safety, and that knowledge is happiness."[3]

Yet he was not to be completely disappointed. Although the general bill did not gain approval, the Assembly passed a resolution directing twenty-four commissioners to prepare specific recommendations for a university (see *1818*). Jefferson was now seventy-four years old, and it was to the establishment of the University of Virginia that he devoted his last years. It was not until 1846 that Virginia made statewide provision for free primary schools, and then only on a permissive basis in the counties.

Jefferson was not an advocate of compulsory school attendance. He did, on the other hand, favor a reading test for citizenship, stipulating in his unsuccessful bill of 1817 that "no person unborn or under the age of twelve years at the passing of this act, and who is *compos mentis,* shall, after the age of fifteen years, be a citizen of this commonwealth until he or she can read readily in some tongue, native or acquired."[4] Unlike some who led the drive for Americanization in our first World War, he did not demand that the reading be in English.

---

[3] Thomas Jefferson to George Ticknor, November 25, 1817.
[4] *Bill for Establishing a System of Public Education,* 1817.

Suggestions for Additional Reading

Honeywell, Roy J. *The Educational Work of Thomas Jefferson*. Cambridge, Massachusetts: Harvard University Press, 1931. Contains the text of *A Bill for the More General Diffusion of Knowledge,* pp. 199–205, and of the 1817 *Bill for Establishing a System of Public Education,* pp. 233–243.

Lee, Gordon C. (ed.). *Crusade Against Ignorance: Thomas Jefferson on Education.* (Classics in Education No. 6.) New York: Bureau of Publications, Teachers College, Columbia University, 1961. Contains the text of *A Bill for the More General Diffusion of Knowledge,* pp. 83–92; of a portion of Query XIV of *Notes on the State of Virginia,* pp. 92–97; and of Jefferson's letter to George Ticknor, November 25, 1817, pp. 112–114.

Padover, Saul K. (ed.). *The Complete Jefferson.* New York: Duell, Sloan & Pearce, Inc., 1943. Contains various writings of Jefferson on education, including the text of *A Bill for the More General Diffusion of Knowledge,* pp. 1048–1054, and of Query XIV of *Notes on the State of Virginia,* pp. 655–669.

The University of the State of New York

MEETING IN THEIR SESSION OF 1784, the legislators of the state of New York pondered the question of how to revive and encourage seminaries of learning, a task that had been assigned to them by Governor George Clinton. The only seminary at their disposal was King's College of New York City, chartered by the crown some thirty years before. With a name that had become politically inappropriate, it had been closed since the outbreak of the War of Independence, but it was still available to be encouraged and revived.

The legislators proceeded not only to revive King's College, partly by renaming it Columbia, but also to fashion a new instrument for higher education in the state. In an act passed on May 1, 1784, they created a corporation with the title of the Regents of the University of the State of New York, authorized to govern Columbia and to establish other schools and colleges. Among the members of the Regents chosen in 1784 were Alexander Hamilton and John Jay.

Thus was created a university that had no campus, no professors, no courses, and no students, although it was empowered by the legislature to grant degrees, including those that might be conferred by any universities in Europe. True, it did have jurisdiction over Columbia College, but the reorganization of that institution was completed by 1787. In that year the legislature, on the recommendation of the Regents, transferred Columbia to a separate board of trustees. Columbia still remained in the broad domain of the Regents, but it now had machinery for direct management of its own affairs.

Meanwhile the academy movement (see *1778*) was spreading to New York, with three petitions for the establishment of such institutions before the legislature in 1787. The original act for the university had authorized it to found schools as well as colleges; now the legislature made this more specific by empowering the Regents to incorporate colleges and academies, to grant financial aids, and to visit and inspect all colleges, academies, and schools in the state. Perhaps of most significance for the future, the new law authorized the Regents to revise courses of study in schools that wanted their pupils admitted to examinations for college. Shortly after the passing of this law, the Regents exercised their new powers by granting charters to Erasmus Hall Academy in Flatbush and Clinton Academy in East Hampton.

The University of the State of New York was off on its long and complicated career as an agency with broad powers for directing higher education and what would later be called secondary education as well. When the state made provision for elementary schools, it vested these in an agency that in 1854 became the State Department of Public Instruction. The confusion and controversy resulting from this division of leadership particularly affected the new institutions called high schools. A so-called act of unification in 1904 resolved some difficulties but created others. Subsequent adjustments brought the Department of Education, an agency created in the act of 1904, more directly into the domain of the Regents. This development was confirmed in an amendment to the state constitution in 1938. Under this amendment, the Regents were defined as the head of the Department of Education, with power to appoint and remove the commissioner of education.

What started in 1784 as a project to revive King's College has become, in effect, the governing body for public and private education in the state. The sovereign authority of the people of the state of New York, from whose constitution and legislature the Regents derive their powers, is physically represented in matters pedagogical by various buildings throughout the state, but particularly by the State Education Building in Albany, a massive structure with an overpowering colonnade and seemingly miles of corridors flanked by offices directing the work of schools.

Many people probably think of the Regents most directly as the agency that administers the Regents' Examinations in secondary schools, a practice widely applauded and deplored since it was started in 1878. The Regents have continued to exercise their function of granting charters for new academies and colleges, although the legislature, acting independently of the Regents, has also exercised its power to grant such charters. No institution in the state has been allowed to grant degrees without a charter from either the legislature or the Regents.

The University of the State of New York should not be confused with the State University of New York, an agency created in 1948 to govern the various institutions of public higher education, namely the state colleges and state universities, plus various specialized institutes and a number of community colleges. This agency was given its own board of trustees, but it was also made part of the overall University of the State of New York, under the Regents' jurisdiction.

Associated with the Regents and their work over this period of nearly two centuries have been some of the most distinguished leaders of American thought and practice in the work of schools. Melvil Dewey, known best for his career in library administration and his scheme for classifying books, served as secretary of the Regents during the turbulent period of high-school expansion of the 1890s. The first commissioner of education under the Act of 1904 was Andrew Sloan Draper, who came to that position from the presidency of the University of Illinois. Frank Pierrepont Graves, who had previously served as dean of the School of Education of the University of Pennsylvania, held the office during the critical decades between 1921 and 1940. Although never directly connected with the Regents, President Nicholas Murray Butler of Columbia University took great interest in matters pertaining to the educational welfare of the state and was actively involved in the controversies surrounding the legislation of 1904.

Suggestions for Additional Reading

Abbott, Frank C. *Government and Higher Education: A Study of the Regents of the University of the State of New York, 1784–1949*. Ithaca, N.Y.: Cornell University Press, 1958.

The University of the State of New York. *Education in New York State 1784–1954*. Albany, N.Y.: The University, 1954.

The Northwest Ordinance

"RELIGION, MORALITY, AND KNOWLEDGE, being necessary to good government and the happiness of mankind, schools and the means of education shall forever be encouraged."[1] With these ringing sentiments, commonplace though they were in much lofty discourse at the time, the Congress of the Confederation recorded its commitment to education in the national destiny of the United States. They occur in one of the last official acts of this Congress, forming the first sentence of Article III of the ordinance "for the Government of the Territory of the United States Northwest of the River Ohio," known usually as The Northwest Ordinance, passed in 1787 on the thirteenth of July.

This document was the culmination of negotiations arising from the cessions of these western lands by Virginia and other states to the United States. It had been preceded by the Land Ordinance of May 20, 1785, which had outlined the plan under which the land was to be surveyed. The Northwest Ordinance of 1787 set forth the details of territorial organization and contained stipulations for the drawing up of states.

The authorship of the famous sentence about "the means of education" is uncertain; probably it was written by Nathan Dane, congressman from Massachusetts, a member of the drafting committee. It was not written, as is sometimes supposed, by Jefferson.

[1] The Northwest Ordinance, July 13, 1787.

One possible way of encouraging schools was through grants of public lands. According to the Land Ordinance of 1785, the new territory was to be surveyed into Congressional townships 6 miles square, each containing lots or sections of 1 square mile (640 acres) each; lot number 16 in each of these townships was reserved for public schools. Evidently little was done about this, for the question was raised anew at the time of Ohio's admission to statehood in 1802; at that time the school grant was reaffirmed. Similar provisions were made for each state admitted to the Union, except Maine and Texas, up to 1850. From then on, new states usually received at least two sections in each township.

States and school districts used and disposed of these lands in various ways. In some cases the lands were quickly sold and the proceeds dissipated. Some states tried to guard against this. The Indiana constitution of 1816, for example, prohibited the sale of any of these lands before 1820. It also stipulated that the proceeds were to be used exclusively for promoting literature and the sciences and for the support of seminaries and public schools.

The land grants obviously constituted a species of what has come to be known as general federal aid to education. In the many debates that have taken place on this topic, the land-grant policy has been frequently invoked as a precedent that could be safely followed. The tendency of the national government, however, has been to grant aids for special purposes, such as those of the Land Grant College Act (see *1862*). It has also moved to the granting of money rather than lands, but the money grants have also been made for special, not general, purposes (see *1917, 1958,* and *1964*).

On the relations between church and state, an attempt was made and only narrowly defeated in 1785 to reserve one section of each township for the support of religion. The Northwest Ordinance of 1787, however, specifically listed religion along with morality and good government as objects to be pursued. Whether this supports religious teaching in public schools, and if so what kind of religious teaching, must be left to each person who reads and interprets the ordinance. It is not clear, furthermore, that the ordinance had public schools in mind. All that it said was schools and the means of education. On the other hand, the Ordinance of 1785 had used the term *public schools* in its grant of lot number 16.

Whatever precedents may have been established by the Ordinance of 1785 and the Northwest Ordinance of 1787 do not render any less difficult the resolution of modern controversies about federal aid or religion in the public schools. Possibly they add to the difficulties. In any case they do not present conclusions binding on the latter decades of the twentieth century. They may be of use in identifying some aspects of American tradition on these matters.

Suggestions for Additional Reading

Commager, Henry Steele (ed.). *Documents of American History.* 6th ed. revised. New York: Appleton-Century-Crofts, Inc., 1958. Contains the text of the Land Ordinance of 1785, pp. 123–124, and of the Northwest Ordinance of 1787, pp. 128–132.

Cubberley, Ellwood P. (ed.). *Readings in Public Education in the United States.* Boston: Houghton Mifflin Company, 1934. Contains the portion of the Indiana constitution dealing with the school lands, pp. 112–113.

Massachusetts Law on
School Districts

THE MASSACHUSETTS LAW "to Provide for the Instruction of Youth, and for the Promotion of Good Education," enacted June 25, 1789, substantially affirmed the old law of 1647, but with modifications. Where the old law had stipulated only reading and writing for the lower schools, the new one added instruction in the English language, "as well as in arithmetic, orthography, and decent behavior."[1] Of more significance for the future of school organization in the United States, it authorized the towns to do what many already had been doing, namely, to define within their boundaries a new kind of school unit, called a district.

School districts represented an adjustment made in response to changing conditions in the towns, these being geographical areas often covering several square miles and governed by town meetings. Toward the end of the seventeenth century, town populations had begun to spread away from the village centers around which they had first clustered. This made it difficult to decide where to hold the town school. The solution was to hold it in different parts of the town during different times of the year, and the term *moving school* thus came into use. The divisions of the town to which it moved were first called squadrons and then districts. During the eighteenth

[1] Massachusetts, *General Laws*, 1789, chap. 19.

century some of the towns allocated to each such district its share of the school funds, presumably to maintain its own school.

While the law of 1789 recognized and authorized the districts, it left them with somewhat uncertain status. A step toward clarification was taken in the law of 1800, which gave the people of a district the right to hold meetings, choose clerks, and lay taxes. Under the law of 1817, school districts became corporations with powers to sue and to be sued. District organization was not required; it remained nonetheless a widespread form of organization in Massachusetts until 1882. In that year a new law abolished the districts and ordered that the towns again assume the functions of school units.

Meanwhile the idea of the school district had spread across much of the United States. Except for the South, where county organization prevailed, the district system, or some variant of it, became the national symbol of educational control, with specific terminology and practice showing differences from state to state. Cities have unified their school systems and in many instances have become single districts. In some states, towns or townships serve as school units. The so-called common district, one not geographically coterminous with other units of government, found and has retained its stronghold in some states of the Middle West.

The great majority of local school units have been small in area, many of them containing only one school. What American folklore has known as the district school, therefore, has been the one-room rural school of the little-red-schoolhouse type. With units tending to be small, there have been a great many of them. As late as the 1940s there were 112,000 school units throughout the land, each with its own governing board; the state of Illinois led with 12,000. School trustees in some states have outnumbered the teachers. Since 1940 there has been much reorganization and the number of units has been greatly reduced. There were still about 26,000 in 1965.

No local unit possesses independent sovereignty or power in matters pertaining to the schools. Sovereignty is held and exercised only by the people of a state, limited in some matters by actions of the federal courts. What the local school unit exercises is delegated authority, usually that of employing and dismissing teachers, laying taxes, and establishing courses of study, but always within the framework of the state constitution and of statutory law. Although the districts in Massachusetts grew up by themselves, they could not continue to exist after the people of the state decided otherwise in 1882.

Still, the local school unit remains one of the most tangible symbols of the principle of decentralization in American government. Probably no other unit has evoked from its constituents so much local fervor and pride. Many matters pertaining to schools will in all probability continue to be dealt with by local units. What our citizens have come to expect, however, is that units be so organized as to provide adequate financial support both locally and from the state, modern buildings and equipment, good teachers, and defensible programs of study.

Suggestions for Additional Reading

Martin, George H. *The Evolution of the Massachusetts Public School System*. New York: D. Appleton and Company, 1894, reprinted 1923.

The New York Free School Society

TWELVE MEN CAME TOGETHER in New York City on February 19, 1805, to consider what might be done about educating the children of the poor, having in mind particularly those who were not then in one of the existing religious or charity schools. They decided to share this concern with the state legislature and were duly incorporated by that body on April 9 as "The Society for establishing a Free School in the City of New York, for the education of such poor children as do not belong to, or are not provided for, by any religious society."[1] Within a month, the society had organized itself with thirteen trustees, headed by De Witt Clinton as President, and had begun to solicit funds, with Clinton's contribution of $200 heading the list.

At this time the state of New York had no provisions for what would later be called public schools. The Regents were empowered to charter colleges, academies, and schools undertaken by private initiative, and even to grant funds to such institutions, but nothing existed for local school systems. The only act in this direction, passed in 1795, had expired in 1800 without being revived.

---

[1] Quoted in William Oland Bourne, *History of the Public School Society of the City of New York* (New York: Wm. Wood & Co., 1870), p. 4.

New York City in 1805, therefore, offered a clear field of action to a philanthropic effort such as this Free School Society, which was following, perhaps, the example set by the organization of similar groups in Philadelphia and Baltimore in 1799. By the end of the year, the society had enough money to begin planning for the opening of its first schools, an event that took place on May 19, 1806. Although this school had only 42 pupils, the trustees, anticipating future growth, decided to adopt the monitorial plan of instruction as developed by Joseph Lancaster in England, under which large numbers could be taught by a few masters, supplemented by pupil assistants.

The first school opened in a small apartment, but was moved in the spring of 1807 to a building described as a tenement and made available to the society by the city. By the end of the year the school had 150 pupils, and it soon reached the tenement's capacity of 250. In 1809, aided by a grant of land from the city, money from the legislature, and donations from the public, the society built its own schoolhouse. At the dedication exercises on December 11, De Witt Clinton delivered a lengthy oration, filled with the pedagogical sentiments of the century that had just passed, yet containing much that would be repeated in the future. "Ignorance," he declared, "is the cause as well as the effect of bad governments, and without the cultivation of our rational powers, we can entertain no just ideas of the obligations of morality or the excellences of religion."[2] Much of the address was devoted to praise of Joseph Lancaster and the monitorial system.

By the year 1824, fifteen years after the dedication of its new building, the Free School Society was well established indeed. It was conducting six schools, with a total attendance of about 5,000 pupils, boys and girls ranging from six to fifteen years of age. State appropriations were coming to it from the Common School Fund that had been established under New York's school law of 1812. The schools took part in the civic life of the times, as, for example,

[2] *Ibid.*, p. 15.

in September, 1824, when School Number Three was visited by General Lafayette, who was received with loud applause and by a parade of school children with banners, one of which proclaimed that education was the basis of good government.

Nevertheless, the society was finding itself confronted by new questions, caused in part by the excellent reputation of the schools it maintained. Many parents, it was reported, wanted their children to go to the society's schools, but not on a charity basis. The society also found itself engaged in controversy with the Bethel Baptist Church over the use made by that institution of the common school funds not only for charity pupils, as was the practice in the other religious schools, but for general expansion of their church school enterprise. This turned into a general controversy over the distribution of the common school funds. The legislature on November 19, 1824, directed the New York City Council to decide which set of schools should receive them. Early in the following year, the council excluded all the religious schools from participation in the funds, thus confining the distribution of state money to the Free School Society and three other, but smaller, philanthropic groups.

Apparently this implied a broader role for the society, and the state legislature in 1826 reorganized it under a new charter. The name was changed to the Public School Society of New York, charged with the duty of providing "so far as their means may extend, for the education of all children in the city of New York not otherwise provided for, whether such children be or not be the proper objects of gratuitous education, and without regard to the religious sect or denomination to which such children or their parents may belong."[3] The society was authorized to make a "moderate" tuition charge, provided that no child be excluded on the ground of ability to pay, and it did so until 1832, at which time all tuition charges were dropped.

The effect of the new charter was to make the society the agency for common schooling in New York City. This did not, however,

[3] *Ibid.*, p. 101.

resolve the question of funds for the religious schools. Between 1840 and 1842, the society found itself again caught up in this controversy, the new occasion of which was the unsuccessful request of the Roman Catholics that religious groups again receive a share of the state school funds.

Probably as a culmination of these controversies, the state legislature on April 9, 1842, created a Board of Education for New York City to develop and administer a system of free and common schools. It specifically excluded from a share in the school funds any schools "in which any religious sectarian doctrine or tenet shall be taught, inculcated, or practised."[4] This did not cut off the funds of the Public School Society, but it created a parallel system. At this time the schools of the society had nearly 25,000 pupils.

The society continued to operate its schools, even opening new ones, but the end was near. In 1848, the legislature forbade the society to open new schools without the permission of the Board of Education; the board had already declared itself against such expansion of the society's activities. Five years later the society decided to end its existence and to transfer its property to the City Council and the board, thus merging its schools with the system of public instruction.

On July 29, 1853, the Committee on Transfer of the Society wrote the final report, anticipating the changeover scheduled for August 1. In this report, the estimate was made that the society had received over 600,000 children in its schools since 1805. "On this day," wrote the committee, "the schools of the Public School Society have closed for the summer vacation; when they open again, their Alma Mater will have ceased to be. New auspices, new school officers to a large extent, and a new system of government and responsibility, will have supervened the ancient order of things. . . . What is to be the result of the change, it is not for us to say. . . . The result is with the almighty Disposer of events."[5]

[4] *Ibid.*, p. 524.
[5] *Ibid.*, p. 593.

Suggestions for Additional Reading

Bourne, William Oland. *History of the Public School Society of the City of New York*. New York: Wm. Wood & Co., 1870. Contains many of the documents pertaining to the society.

McCluskey, Neil G. (ed.). *Catholic Education in America: A Documentary History*. New York: Bureau of Publications, Teachers College, Columbia University, 1964. Contains the Petition of the Catholics of New York for a Portion of the Common School Fund (1840), pp. 65–77.

The Rockfish Gap Meeting
on the University of Virginia

At the end of July, 1818, Thomas Jefferson set off on horseback from his home in Monticello to attend a meeting in Rockfish Gap, twenty-eight miles away, planning because of his infirmities to take two days for the trip. He was going in his capacity as one of the twenty-four commissioners directed by the Virginia Assembly earlier that year to prepare recommendations for a University. This was for Jefferson a happy occasion indeed, a tangible step toward a goal he had pursued for many of his seventy-four years.

The commissioners came together on Saturday, August first, and remained in session "at the tavern" until Tuesday, by which time they had agreed on a general report. Only twenty-one signatures appeared; the other three commissioners presumably were absent. The report was based on a draft that Jefferson had brought with him to the meeting. This was not presumption on his part; he and James Madison had been given this assignment by their colleagues. Madison, however, had urged Jefferson to go ahead on his own. It may be taken, then, that Jefferson was substantially the author of the Rockfish Gap report as it stood approved.

Although this report has gained its fame from the lofty ideology of higher education therein expressed, it began on a practical note, namely, the decision to locate the university on the site of Central College in the village, now the city, of Charlottesville. Jefferson's advocacy of this site probably reflected his desire to be as close to his creation as possible; it was only three miles from the heights of Monticello and could be seen from there on a clear day. The report next stated the plan for the campus and its buildings, spelled out with Jeffersonian love for details, complete with estimates of cost.

With these tangible points disposed of, Jefferson turned to the question that has engaged all planners of curriculum, that of the purposes or what he called the objects of schooling. Still concerned, as he had been in 1779, with the general enlightenment of the electorate, he dealt first with the objects of primary education. Six of these were given in detail and then summarized as that of instructing "the mass of our citizens in these, their rights, interests and duties, as men and citizens," including the choice of their representatives and leaders.[1]

The aims of the "higher branches" of education were then stated as follows:

To form the statesmen, legislators and judges, on whom public prosperity and individual happiness are so much to depend;

To expound the principles and structure of government, the laws which regulate the intercourse of nations, those formed municipally for our own government, and a sound spirit of legislation, which, banishing all arbitrary and unnecessary restraint on individual action, shall leave us free to do whatever does not violate the equal rights of another;

To harmonize and promote the interests of agriculture, manufactures and commerce, and by well informed views of public economy to give a free scope to the public industry;

To develop the reasoning faculties of our youth, enlarge their minds, cultivate their morals, and instill into them the precepts of virtue and order;

To enlighten them with mathematical and physical sciences, which advance the arts, and administer to the health, the subsistence, and comforts of human life;

[1] Report of the Commissioners Appointed to Fix the Site of the University of Virginia, August 4, 1818.

And, generally, to form them to habits of reflection and correct action, rendering them examples of virtue to others, and of happiness within themselves.

To accomplish these aims, Jefferson proposed a curriculum in ten categories: ancient languages; modern languages, with French, Spanish, Italian, German, and Anglo-Saxon; pure mathematics; physico-mathematics, including such divisions as mechanics, statics, acoustics, and optics; physics, or natural philosophy, with chemistry and mineralogy; botany and zoology; anatomy and medicine; government and history; municipal law; and a group called "Ideology," made up by "General Grammar, Ethics, Rhetoric, Belles Lettres, and the fine arts."

Some of the foregoing classifications may sound strange to the modern ear; evidently Jefferson feared they might not be clear to his contemporaries, for he included a glossary of terms in the text of the report. In this he defined "Ideology" as "the doctrine of thought." Probably most astounding to modern academicians would be his assumption that each of the foregoing groups was "within the powers of a single professor."

Even with the glossary, Jefferson felt compelled to explain some of his recommendations at length, including the questionable identification of Anglo-Saxon as a modern tongue. The study of ancient languages, he pointed out, would be of an advanced nature only, this in part to guard against the presence in the university of "the intrusions and the noisy turbulence of a multitude of small boys." Here he returned to his 1779 proposal for grammar schools, now calling them "district schools or colleges," where the rudiments of the classics would be taught. What he intended was that youth come to the university at the age of fifteen. He concluded his explanations of the curriculum with a recommendation that gymnastics, military exercises, and the manual arts, plus "the innocent arts" of dancing, music, and drawing, be provided as what we might call extra-class activities, but not included in the formal program of studies.

At the end of the report, Jefferson turned again to immediate and practical concerns, stipulating the duties and powers of the "visitors" who would constitute the governing board. He offered suggestions on discipline, expressing his disapproval of "corporal punishments, and servile humiliations." The document was closed by a number of details affecting the transfer of the property of Central College to the new institution.

Six months later, on January 25, 1819, the assembly passed an act establishing the University of Virginia along the lines proposed. For the first time in his long career, Jefferson had succeeded in carrying one of his ideas about education through the assembly of his commonwealth. The act even included his curriculum in condensed form, but added to it the principles of agriculture, a subject he had alluded to in his glossary as a branch of chemistry.

Appropriately, Jefferson was made rector of the Board of Visitors. He proceeded at once to carry the plan into effect. Spending much time at the site itself (and gazing at it from Monticello when he could not be there in person), Jefferson supervised the creation of the campus and the recruitment of the staff, giving special care to the library. In March, 1825, one month before his eighty-first birthday, Jefferson realized in the formal opening of the university the culmination of his vision for the higher studies.

One part of his bill of 1779 was missing from the Rockfish Gap report, the provision for complete tuition and support of youth of genius who could not otherwise afford to pursue advanced studies. Perhaps he felt this would jeopardize the goal of achieving the university itself. In this he was probably correct. After all, he had tried without success as late as 1817 to carry a bill with such provisions through the assembly.

The University of Virginia was created as a state university and has remained such. Even with Harvard excluded from this category, Virginia was not the first state university in our country. Several had been opened before the Rockfish Gap report, the earliest of these so recognized being those of North Carolina in 1795 and Georgia in 1801.

Suggestions for Additional Reading

Davis, Richard Beale. *Intellectual Life in Jefferson's Virginia 1790–1830.* Chapel Hill, N.C.: The University of North Carolina Press, 1964.

Honeywell, Roy J. *The Educational Work of Thomas Jefferson.* Cambridge, Mass.: Harvard University Press, 1931. Contains the Rockfish Gap report, pp. 248–260.

Lee, Gordon C. (ed.). *Crusade against Ignorance: Thomas Jefferson on Education.* (Classics in Education No. 6.) New York: Bureau of Publications, Teachers College, Columbia University, 1961. Contains the Rockfish Gap report, pp. 114–133.

Peterson, Merrill D, *The Jefferson Image in the American Mind.* New York: Oxford University Press, 1960.

The Boston English Classical School

CITIZENS OF BOSTON, assembled in town meeting at Faneuil Hall, voted on January 15, 1821, to accept a recommendation made by their school committee for the establishment of what was called an "English Classical School." Five months later the masters opened the school for 102 students in a brick building on the site of what is now the extension of the State House. These events are regarded conventionally as the beginning of the free and public high school in the United States.

The recommendation made by the school committee was based on a report submitted in October, 1820, by a subcommittee of five members, including two clergymen, an editor, a merchant, and a future judge. At this time the Boston school system consisted of the free Latin School, allegedly founded 186 years before, and the free schools of reading and writing in the English tongue. These reading and writing schools, according to the subcommittee, did not go far enough, and the report contended that "a parent who wishes to give a child an education that shall fit him for an active life, and shall serve as a foundation for eminence in his profession, whether Mercantile or Mechanical, is under the necessity of giving him a different education from any which our public schools can now furnish."[1]

---

[1] Report of the Subcommittee of the Boston School Committee, October 26, 1820.

This may have represented indirect criticism of the free Public Latin School, although that institution was not mentioned by name.

"Hence many children," continued the subcommittee, "are separated from their parents and sent to private academies in this vicinity, to acquire that instruction, which cannot be obtained at the public seminaries. Thus, many parents, who contribute largely to the support of these institutions, are subjected to heavy expense for the same object in other towns." Having established to its satisfaction the reasons for an English school, the subcommittee proceeded to outline a three-year curriculum and to propose a salary of $1,500 for a principal and a total of $2,500 for the salaries of a submaster and two ushers. "No money can be better expended," concluded the report, "than that which is appropriated to the support of public schools."

The three-year course of study was designed for boys admitted at not less than twelve years of age. Candidates for admission were to be "subject to a strict examination," based on reading, writing, English grammar "in all its branches," and arithmetic to simple proportion. Once admitted, the students would pursue a strenuous program indeed, ranging from such bread-and-butter subjects as navigation and surveying to the lofty heights of moral and political philosophy and to the writings of "the most approved authors," and including algebra, geometry, logic, and history along the way. The actual curriculum of the school followed the recommendations of the report, adding to these, however, the study of bookkeeping, natural theology, and Paley's *Evidences of Christianity*.

Three years after the school was opened, the Boston School Committee gave it a new building and referred to it as the English High School, the name it has carried since except for a brief period in the early 1830s. Why the name was changed is not known; possibly there were objections to the use of the term *classical* by a school that taught no Latin or Greek. Another unanswered question is where the committee got the term *high school;* according to one interpretation, it was taken from an institution by that name in Edinburgh, Scotland.

Under the leadership of a series of vigorous masters, particularly Thomas Sherwin, between 1837 and 1869, the school developed a strong reputation for academic excellence. There was, however, no rapid increase in enrollments, as might have been expected from the alleged public demand it had been created to meet. By 1850, the English and the Latin Schools had about 200 students each, an odd state of affairs in view of the popular and aristocrat images of the two institutions. Perhaps the examinations for admission to the English School had been made too strict! In any case the enrollments of both schools increased markedly during the secondary-school upsurge after 1890. By 1920, however, the English High School had become much larger than the Latin School, numbering some 2,200 students as contrasted with slightly over 1,000 for the latter.

It was assumed during the early period that the English High School did not prepare students for college, although the subcommittee's report of 1820 had been silent on this point. Obviously it did not through its formal curriculum prepare students for the usual entrance examinations in Latin and Greek. As these requirements were modified, graduates of the English High School did go to college; the school also added instruction in Latin and in modern languages, in addition to other subjects not contemplated by the subcommittee's report. Eventually the English High School offered several courses of study or curricula, some of which were designated as college preparatory.

The subcommittee back in 1820 had sternly designated the school as one for "boys exclusively." In 1826, the school committee opened the High School for Girls, with 130 students admitted out of 286 who took the examinations for entrance. The popularity of this school created problems, both of accommodating the numbers of girls who wanted to come and of placating the parents of those who were not admitted. Within two years the committee decided to solve the problems by closing the school. It was reopened in 1852.

Suggestions for Additional Reading

Centenary Committee of the English High School Association. *One Hundred Years of the English High School of Boston.* Boston: The Committee, 1924.

Cubberley, Ellwood P. (ed.). *Readings in Public Education in the United States.* Boston: Houghton Mifflin Company, 1934. Contains the subcommittee's report of 1820, pp. 228–230.

Massachusetts Law on High Schools

PERHAPS WITH THE BOSTON ENGLISH HIGH SCHOOL IN MIND, the Commonwealth of Massachusetts established a new policy for secondary education in a law dated March 10, 1827. The law required that every city, town, or district with 500 householders or more maintain a master who could teach American history, bookkeeping by single entry, geometry, surveying, and algebra. Beyond this, it stipulated that in cities or towns of 4,000 or more inhabitants the masters also be able to teach Latin and Greek, history (presumably general history), rhetoric, and logic. The term *high school,* however, did not appear in the law.

Under these provisions, the Latin grammar school of a community could be absorbed into a new institution. This part of the law of 1827 represented the culmination of past changes in the original requirement for the grammar schools. Where the law of 1647 had required such a school in a community with 100 householders, that of 1789 had raised the number to 200. In 1824, all communities of fewer than 5,000 people had been excused from the requirement; this had left only 7 communities to which the requirement applied.

By 1840, Massachusetts had 26 schools of the kind envisioned by the law of 1827. Most of them were called high schools. Some were divided into separate schools for boys and girls; others were coeducational. There was variation also in the relationship of these new institutions to the grammar schools. Boston, for example, chose to keep its separate grammar school, the Public Latin School for boys, while others took the opportunity provided by the law to maintain a high school that taught Latin and Greek. Each community had its own pattern of development.

It should be kept in mind, however, that a school often meant one schoolmaster, probably a long-suffering one, required as he now might be to handle subjects ranging from surveying to Greek. Mercifully, the law required him to be competent in bookkeeping only by single entry.

The growth of the public high school, even in Massachusetts, was slow and uncertain. Apparently the law of 1827 was not strictly enforced, and it suffered from legislative tinkering that provided exemptions for some of the towns and districts where it should have applied. Outside of Massachusetts there were only isolated instances of high schools before 1850, and most of these were in the New England states. One notable exception was the Philadelphia Central High School, established in 1837. Statistics on public high schools for this period, in fact for the entire period up to 1890, are notoriously unreliable.

Strangely enough, the slow development of public high schools before 1850 was accompanied by the almost reckless expansion of academies. Many of the academies, however, were semipublic institutions, chartered by their states, and in some cases receiving grants of public funds. The machinery of starting an academy was probably less cumbersome than that of starting a public high school. State legislatures in this period tended to provide a variety of financial aids through literary and educational funds; local communities were more reluctant to embark on enterprises to be supported largely by local taxes, even when required to do so by state law.

It has been contended also by some observers of the high schools in Massachusetts that academies were more flexible in their administrative policies and in efforts to meet the circumstances of students.

So far as the high schools were concerned, this is borne out in part by the report of the school committee of Lowell, Massachusetts, in 1851, in which the local high school was declared out of step with prevailing practice. Other high schools, said this report, had prescribed courses of study with annual admission only. Lowell, however, left the choice of studies to the students and admitted new students each term. "Is our practice," asked the committee, "founded in wisdom?"[1] They decided not. The following year Lowell, too, had prescribed courses of study, one called Classical, the other English.

The dual program adopted by Lowell was then emerging as a familiar pattern and was destined to become widespread throughout the rest of the nineteenth century. English courses of study followed substantially the outline of subjects at the Boston English High School, but with numerous variations in the terms used for the many sciences and philosophies that adorned the printed announcements. Classical courses of study came to include little more than Latin, Greek, and mathematics, with a little ancient history. Not all high schools, however, adopted the dual program. Many small ones continued to have a single course of study. This usually meant that all students had to take Latin if it was offered.

After 1850, the development of high schools picked up speed, especially in New York, Pennsylvania, and the Middle West. It has been estimated that there were about 300 high schools in the country just before the Civil War, of which more than one-fourth were in Massachusetts. Chicago started its first high school in 1856, equipped with three courses, Classical, English, and Normal, the latter for the training of teachers. A year later it pointed with pride to an enrollment of 151 students. High schools were found almost exclusively in cities until after the Civil War, and for long thereafter were regarded mostly as city institutions. Not all cities, however, had them. New York City, although it had a public college (called by some a secondary school), did not establish public high schools until 1897.

---

[1] Quoted in John Elbert Stout, *The Development of High-School Curricula in the North Central States from 1860 to 1918* (Chicago: The University of Chicago, 1918), p. 6.

Suggestions for Additional Reading

Cubberley, Ellwood P. (ed.). *Readings in Public Education in the United States.* Boston: Houghton Mifflin Company, 1934. Contains the law of 1827, pp. 231–232, and other documents on early high schools, pp. 232–239.

Grizzell, Emit Duncan. *Origin and Development of the High School in New England before 1865.* New York: The Macmillan Company, 1923.

Pennsylvania Free School Law

PENNSYLVANIA FOLLOWED THE TREND of the times by enacting a new school law on April 1, 1834. The immediate result was a conflict that spread widely throughout the state. Dramatically involved in this conflict was a young legislator named Thaddeus Stevens, destined later to become one of the most controversial figures in the larger domain of American history as well.

The law of 1834 was the successful outcome of a seven-year campaign of persuasion conducted by the Philadelphia Society for the Promotion of Public Schools. Before 1834 Pennsylvania had been managing its pedagogical affairs under the old law of 1809, known as the Pauper-School Law, although the term *pauper* did not appear in its text. Under the law of 1809, the counties had paid the school bills of children whose parents were unable to do so. The schools themselves were mainly those sponsored by churches.

Under the new law, the existing wards, townships, and boroughs of the state were designated as school districts. Each of these was to decide early in the fall of 1834 whether to organize free schools; districts that rejected the free schools were to continue under the law of 1809. Of the 987 districts thus created, 502 chose the free schools, 264 rejected them, and 221 took no action. The northern tier of counties, presumably influenced by settlers from New England, went most heavily for the free schools.

The bitter discussion that accompanied these local decisions spread into the political domain, and the new school law became a major issue in the election of the new legislature scheduled to convene at the end of the year. Opponents of the law included those who feared it would hurt the church schools, some who saw injustice in taxing people for the children of others, and one critic who viewed the law as providing teaching jobs for men too lazy to work for an honest living. Defenders of the law accused their opponents of narrow-mindedness and prejudice.

It was assumed that most of the legislators who gathered at Harrisburg on December 3, 1834, were determined to repeal the law. Governor Wolf ardently defended it in his message. Nevertheless, the opponents went speedily to work, backed up, they felt, by 32,000 signatures attached to 538 petitions for repeal. The repeal bill passed the senate, but encountered opposition in the house, where a substitute was voted that amended the law without repealing it. According to the advocates of free schools, these amendments made the law better. This substitute bill was accepted by the senate, probably because the members of that body realized the futility of trying to get the house to accept outright repeal.

It was during the house debate that Thaddeus Stevens made his famous speech against the repeal bill. Stevens had come from Vermont, presumably motivated by the New England passion for schooling. He was a graduate of Dartmouth, who after some teaching in an academy at York, Pennsylvania, had turned to the practice of law.

Early in his speech, Stevens offered the usual testimony to the need for education in free governments. Against those who objected to paying taxes for other people's children, he argued that most people never used jails, but still paid taxes for them. Warming up to his subject, he charged his opponents with "the vile arts of unprincipled demagogues" and with catering to prejudice. "I do not," he declared, "charge this on any particular party. Unfortunately, almost the only spot on which all parties meet in union, is this ground of common infamy!"[1]

[1] Quoted in James Pyle Wickersham, *A History of Education in Pennsylvania* (Lancaster, Pa.: published by the author, 1886), pp. 334–335.

Never celebrated for his tact, Stevens congratulated the governor on his opposition to repeal, especially since this would atone for many errors and "deep political sins" committed by that chief executive in times past. From his appraisal of the governor, he moved to the dangers confronting the backers of the law of 1834, stating that the "war-club and battle-axe of savage ignorance" were only little less than the scimitar of the Saracens had been to Richard the Lion-Hearted. More positively, he gave eloquent voice to the growing American conviction that schooling not be denied to the poor.

According to those present at the time, it was this speech that swayed the house and saved the law of 1834 from repeal. One of these observers wrote many years later that Stevens had electrified the house. In any case, this speech made Stevens a hero to the advocates of free schools at that time, some of whom in Reading bestowed upon him a copy of it printed on silk. It also made him a long-time hero to succeeding generations of Pennsylvania schoolmen. Although his subsequent role in the Reconstruction Congress has been subject to wide differences in historical judgment, to the *Pennsylvania School Journal* in 1906 he remained "one of the grandest characters of the Civil War" and "a man who is held in high honor everywhere in Pennsylvania."[2]

The successful resistance to repeal in the legislature of 1834–1835 did not immediately resolve the issues. Governor Wolf was defeated for re-election in the fall of 1835, probably because he had opposed repeal; the anti-free-school forces supported his successful opponent, Joseph Ritner. They evidently misjudged their man. Instead of attacking the free schools, the new governor recommended and obtained a greatly increased appropriation for state financial aids to the local districts. The legislature that had been elected with him once more revised and, in the opinion of many, improved the law of 1834. It was under a provision of the revised law that the Philadelphia Central High School was organized in 1837.

2 "Editorial," *Pennsylvania School Journal*, LV (November, 1906), 234.

Suggestions for Additional Reading

Cubberley, Ellwood P. (ed.). *Readings in Public Education in the United States.* Boston: Houghton Mifflin Company, 1934. Contains the law of 1809, the preamble to the law of 1834, portions of the Stevens speech, and other documents on Pennsylvania school history, pp. 173–181.

Wickersham, James Pyle. *A History of Education in Pennsylvania.* Lancaster, Pa.: published by the author, 1886. Contains extensive quotations from the Stevens speech.

The McGuffey Eclectic Readers

SINCE COLONIAL TIMES, books have done much to determine the nature of American schooling. It was from the 3,000,000 or so copies of *The New England Primer* published and sold during the eighteenth and early nineteenth centuries that many young Americans did their first reading. Noah Webster published his famous speller in 1783; the income from this book and his other school texts provided him with leisure to write his dictionary. Most widely known of all American schoolbooks, however, have been the McGuffey readers, the first of which was brought forth by Truman and Smith, a Cincinnati publishing house, in 1836.

Born in western Pennsylvania in 1800, William Holmes McGuffey grew up in the frontier environment of Trumbull County, Ohio. He acquired his early education at home and in private study with a clergyman of Youngstown. After attending an academy, he entered Washington College, Pennsylvania, taking his A.B. degree there in 1826. He was appointed Professor of Ancient Languages at Miami College, Oxford, Ohio, in the same year.

There are two versions of how McGuffey came to the writing of his famous series of books. In one, he took his idea and a manuscript to Smith, of Truman and Smith; in the other, Smith came to him. The intermediary, according to the second version, was Calvin Stowe, professor in the Lane Seminary of Cincinnati, with whom McGuffey had become acquainted in the Western Literary Institute, an association of teachers.

Smith had allegedly tried to persuade Catherine Beecher, daughter of Lyman Beecher, the seminary's president, to undertake the series. This brought in Stowe, who was then courting Catherine's sister Harriet, his future wife and the author-to-be of *Uncle Tom's Cabin*. The man for the job, Stowe told Smith, was the young professor at Miami. In any case, McGuffey already had prepared or would soon prepare the manuscript for the *First Eclectic Reader*. Truman and Smith published it along with the second reader in 1836.

These were not, in spite of their titles, beginning readers. A year later McGuffey brought out his *Primer* to serve this purpose, adding at that time the third and fourth readers. Like Webster, he produced a speller, which served also as a beginning reading book. The fifth reader apeared in 1844, the sixth in 1857. He completed the series in 1863 with a reader for high schools. On some of these books (accounts vary as to which ones), he had the help of his younger brother, Alexander Hamilton McGuffey.

Along with his writing, William Holmes McGuffey pursued a varied academic career. He moved in quick succession from Miami to the presidency of Cincinnati College, the presidency of Ohio University at Athens, and the faculty of Woodward College, or high school, in Cincinnati. In 1841 he became Professor of Natural Philosophy at the University of Virginia and remained there until his death in 1873.

Unlike Webster, McGuffey did not profit much from his books. He received a total sum of $1,000 for the first four readers, plus fees for revision, and a small annuity from the publishers until his death. The books successively became the property of various publishing houses, ending up in 1890 with the American Book Company.

Almost certainly, neither McGuffey nor Smith anticipated in 1836 the sales triumph these books were to achieve. There were plenty of competitors, old and new, but McGuffey outstripped them all. According to estimates, 122,000,000 copies of the books were sold by 1920.

The readers contained both poetry and prose, usually short selections from a great variety of sources. Those for younger children had stories about animals, games, family life, and nature; the fourth, fifth, and sixth books were anthologies of much familiar literature. Among the American writers included were Lyman Beecher, Catherine Beecher, Whittier, Bryant, and Hawthorne. England was represented by Shakespeare, Goldsmith, Lamb, Byron, Thackeray, and many others.

Lofty pronouncements have been made about the effects of these books on the ethical values of the nineteenth-century American way of life. Obviously McGuffey did have strong convictions about the moral aim in education. These he shared with educators of all times and places. His books, however, dealt not only with morals, but with manners. Perhaps they were aimed also at smoothing off the rough edges of behavior in communities not too far removed from their frontier days.

During the first part of the present century there arose what might be called a McGuffey cult, representing in part nostalgia for a romanticized American past. One of the leaders in this movement was Henry Ford, who had the sets reprinted and distributed to fellow enthusiasts in the 1920s. More recently they have been taken up by some who are critical of modern readers and modern schools. To these critics the books symbolize not only the virtues from which the nation has allegedly departed, but also the use of good, solid literature, as contrasted with what the critics regard as the pallid adventures of boys and girls with their pets on grandfather's farm.

Some have admired the pedagogical devices used in the readers, such as drill work in pronunciation and the use of inflection in speech, along with vocabulary definitions and historical and biographical notes. There was also plenty of controversy over the teaching of reading in McGuffey's own times; this is a matter on which strong feelings will probably always be held and expressed.

Suggestions for Additional Reading

Carpenter, Charles. *History of American Schoolbooks*. Philadelphia: University of Pennsylvania Press, 1963.

Cubberley, Ellwood P. (ed.). *Readings in Public Education in the United States*. Boston: Houghton Mifflin Company, 1934. Contains documents on textbooks in the eighteenth and nineteenth centuries, pp. 46–62 and 266–280.

Ford, Paul Leicester (ed.). *The New-England Primer*. (Classics in Education No. 16.) New York: Bureau of Publications, Teachers College, Columbia University, 1964.

McGuffey's Fifth Eclectic Reader, 1879 Edition. With an introduction by Henry Steele Commager. New York: The New American Library of World Literature, Inc., 1962.

McGuffey's Sixth Eclectic Reader, 1879 Edition. With an introduction by Henry Steele Commager. New York: The New American Library of World Literature, Inc., 1962.

Minnich, Harvey C. *William Holmes McGuffey and His Readers*. New York: American Book Company, 1936.

Nietz, John. *Old Textbooks*. Pittsburgh: University of Pittsburgh Press, 1961.

Horace Mann and the Massachusetts State Board of Education

THE MASSACHUSETTS LEGISLATURE, ever restless in pursuit of the pedagogical good, created the State Board of Education on April 20, 1837. This turned out to be a momentous decision indeed. What made it such was that the post as secretary to the board was offered to and accepted by a forty-one-year-old lawyer named Horace Mann.

Although he supported the bill as a member of the state senate, Horace Mann did not seek the appointment as secretary. In fact, he tried to avoid it. He had done well in politics. His law practice was both prosperous and promising. The board itself was given no power, and its function was to be that of influencing public opinion and informing the legislature through reports. Nevertheless, Mann took the job and with it fashioned both a new career for himself and a new image of the destinies of American schools.

From his boyhood days on a farm in the town of Franklin, Massachusetts, he had relentlessly sought education for himself. With little formal schooling, he entered Brown University in 1816. He took his degree in 1819 and served on its faculty for two years as a tutor in Latin and Greek. He had the usual passion of a New Englander for education. To this he added some ideas of his own, drawing perhaps on the impulse for humanitarian reform then beginning to emerge throughout the country.

The task before him was that of dramatizing the mission of the schools. This might have seemed a strange assignment in a state famed for its educational leadership. The New England passion for education, however, did not always show itself through financial support of public schools. According to many, Massachusetts had allowed its schools to decline. Whether this was so or not, it was Horace Mann's responsibility to goad the state into improvement. Sounding this note in his first report, issued in 1837, he scourged his fellow citizens for what he called their apathy toward the common schools.

In his subsequent reports, turned out at the rate of one a year until his resignation in 1848, Mann continued to hammer away at the obligation of communities to support good schools. To this familiar theme he added technical discussions about such matters as classroom teaching, school discipline, and the training of teachers. His *Seventh Annual Report* (1843) was based on his tour of Europe and included his favorable judgment on the effective teaching and absence of harsh discipline in the Prussian schools. This drew a sharp retort in the form of a 144-page pamphlet from 31 angry schoolmasters of Boston. The resulting controversy spread his fame far beyond New England.

Still, his chief interest and delight lay in discussions of the ideology of education, a subject he pursued especially in his last three reports, numbered ten through twelve. Free schools had become for him virtually a matter of religious conviction; to defend them he appealed to the idea of absolute moral law, a popular feature of much nineteenth-century American thought.

"I believe," he wrote in his *Tenth Annual Report* (1846), "in the existence of a great, immutable principle of natural law, or natural ethics,—a principle antecedent to all human institutions and incapable of being abrogated by any ordinances of man,—a principle of divine origin, clearly legible in the ways of Providence as those ways are manifested in the order of nature and in the history of the race,—which proves the *absolute right* of every human being that comes into the world to an education; and which, of course, proves the correlative duty of every government to see that the means of education are provided for all."[1]

Like other reformers in this period, Horace Mann suffered much from the tragic evidences of poverty and injustice about him. Always on the side of social stability and orderly progress, he rejected direct attack on established institutions and abhorred violence. It was the schools, he felt, that would lead to the betterment of human life, largely by equipping people to help themselves.

"Education, then, beyond all devices of human origin," he wrote in his twelfth and last report (1848), "is the great equalizer of the conditions of men—the balance wheel of the social machinery. . . . It does better than to disarm the poor of their hostility towards the rich; it prevents being poor."[2] In this he voiced his criticism of popular sentiment about free schools at that time, namely that schooling would prevent social disorder by making the poor contented. What he wanted was discontent, but expressed along orderly lines.

In these twelve reports, Horace Mann pronounced his judgments on a vast range of questions in education. About some of these pronouncements, such as those he made on phrenology, his admirers have tended to be apologetic. Other views of his were still being invoked as late as the seventh decade of the twentieth century. Although he rejected what he called sectarian religion in the schools, he believed in the school reading of the Bible without comment (see *1963*). He ardently supported free public schools, but defended the right of private schools to exist. Like Jefferson and others, he stressed the need for popular enlightenment under free government.

After resigning as secretary to the board in 1848, Horace Mann

---

[1] *Tenth Annual Report* (1846), p. 112.
[2] *Twelfth Annual Report* (1848), pp. 59–60.

turned back to politics and then to higher education. As a member of the House of Representatives from Massachusetts, he took part in the conflict over slavery. Like other antislavery men he turned with bitter disappointment from Daniel Webster after the latter's advocacy of the Compromise of 1850 in his Seventh of March Speech. On this occasion he referred to Webster as Lucifer descending from heaven. He closed his political career with an unsuccessful effort to become governor of Massachusetts in 1852. The following year he became president of the newly-founded Antioch College at Yellow Springs, Ohio.

Antioch and Horace Mann seemed made for each other. The college was designed to be nonsectarian but based on the Bible, coeducational, and free from racial discrimination. Although president, Mann was able to teach some courses himself, covering such fields as political economy, moral philosophy, natural theology, and Bible. Still, there were difficulties, mainly financial ones, that marred these last years of his career. When he died on August 2, 1859, he had given to the cause of Antioch College six years of dedicated service and was full of zeal for its future.

It is always difficult to evaluate the specific accomplishments of those who devote themselves mainly to persuasion. Horace Mann has been credited by many with arresting a downhill trend allegedly taking place in the schools of Massachusetts. Perhaps his greatest contribution was the selfless example he provided of devotion to the cause of education. His second wife, the former Mary Peabody of Salem, shared his enthusiasms for the cause; her sister Sophia, the wife of Nathaniel Hawthorne, predicted that Horace and Mary Mann's first child would begin to talk by quoting a school report.[3] Devotee that he was, Horace Mann undoubtedly amused and possibly bored many of his contemporaries. Such appears to be the fate of reformers. Undaunted by this, he exhorted his students at Antioch to be ashamed to die until they had won some victory for humanity.

---

[3] Reported in Louise Hall Tharp, *The Peabody Sisters of Salem* (Boston: Little, Brown and Company, 1950), p. 175.

Suggestions for Additional Reading

Cremin, Lawrence A. (ed.). *The Republic and the School: Horace Mann on the Education of Free Men.* (Classics in Education No. 1.) New York: Bureau of Publications, Teachers College, Columbia University, 1957. Contains portions of the twelve reports.

Curti, Merle. *The Social Ideas of American Educators.* Paterson, N.J.: Pageant Books, 1959, pp. 101–138. Originally published by Charles Scribner's Sons, New York, 1935.

Horace Mann League of America and the Hugh Birch-Horace Mann Fund of the National Education Association. *Annual Reports* (1837–1848). Facsimile reprints of the twelve annual reports in separate pamphlets. Washington, D.C., undated.

Tharp, Louise Hall. *The Peabody Sisters of Salem.* Boston: Little, Brown and Company, 1950.

Tharp, Louise Hall. *Until Victory: Horace Mann and Mary Peabody.* Boston: Little, Brown and Company, 1953.

First State Normal School, Lexington, Massachusetts

LEXINGTON, MASSACHUSETTS, is the site not only of a famous battle, but also of the first state normal school in our country. It was opened on July 3, 1839. The opening was not impressive. Only three students appeared, and it rained. What took place on that occasion, nonetheless, was the birth of a new institution, one with which, in the minds of many, the training of elementary-school teachers would come almost exclusively, but not accurately, to be identified.

In this period, teachers in the common schools came usually from academies. This did not mean they had taken what came to be known as a teacher-training course. Mostly they took what the academy offered and then presented themselves to school committees for certificates.

Back in 1823, however, a minister named Samuel R. Hall had opened an academy at Concord, Vermont, to which he added a course in the art of teaching and provision for some practice in the art. Seven years later he opened a teacher-training course in the Phillips Andover Academy (see *1778*), having in the meantime published a book called *Lectures on Schoolkeeping*. The idea spread to New York and by 1835 there were five academies in that state with courses called principles of teaching.

There was some precedent, then, for the idea of providing special training for those who planned to teach. What distinguished Lexington from the earlier ventures was its creation by the state. It was the result of a campaign led by Massachusetts citizens who were impressed by reports on the teacher-training seminaries of Prussia.

One of the most famous of these reports came from Victor Cousin, a French councilor of state, who had visited Prussia in 1831 under the direction of the French minister of public instruction and ecclesiastical affairs. This report, translated into English with the title *Report on the State of Public Instruction in Prussia,* was widely circulated and read in Great Britain and in the United States. Another influential document, *Report on Elementary Instruction in Europe,* was prepared for the Ohio legislature in 1837 by Calvin Stowe, the man who had reportedly suggested McGuffey as the man to do the readers.

Among those in Massachusetts who urged the creation of state institutions along the lines of the Prussian seminaries were Charles Brooks, a clergyman of Hingham; James G. Carter, a teacher and prominent writer on education; Edmund Dwight, a Boston merchant; Samuel R. Hall, who had started teacher-training work in academies; and Horace Mann. Brooks made a trip to Prussia and on his return delivered many speeches in Massachusetts on behalf of the idea.

In 1838, Dwight offered to contribute $10,000 to what he termed the qualifying of teachers, provided the state would match this amount. This was quickly done. It was left up to Horace Mann and the State Board to devise a plan and put it to work. The school at Lexington, under the headship of a Harvard graduate named Cyrus Peirce, was the result.

Why the institution was called a normal school is not clear. The idea for the school had come from Prussia, but the term *normal* was of French derivation. Once applied, the name proved tenacious indeed.

Although the school at Lexington had only twelve students during its first quarter, the state quickly opened two more such schools, one at Barre, in September, 1839, and one at Bridgewater the following year. Entrants were required to be seventeen years old, if boys, and sixteen, if girls, and to pass an examination in what were called the common branches, namely, orthography, reading, writing, English grammar, geography, and arithmetic. Those who planned to teach in Massachusetts received free tuition. The course of study was first one year in length, later increased to two.

At the dedication of the Barre Normal School, September 4, 1839, Governor Edward Everett, formerly Professor of Greek at Harvard and the future orator of Gettysburg, was asked to give the major address. In his presentation he stated what had undoubtedly been agreed upon among the backers of the plan as the essentials of teacher training: (1) a careful review of the common branches, with the end of having the teacher "know things in a masterly way, curiously, nicely, and in their reasons"; (2) what he called the "peculiar art of teaching"; (3) the best methods of governing a school; and (4) "a school of practice, in which, under the direction of the principal of the school, the young teacher may have the benefit of actual exercise in the business of instruction."[1]

The growth of normal schools, like that of high schools, was slow at first. In Massachusetts there was some uncertainty about where the schools should be located. Lexington's was moved to West Newton and then to Framingham; the one at Barre was shifted to Westfield. Bridgewater's stayed where it was, and a fourth school was added at Salem in 1854. The records of 1856 showed that the four schools had 332 students, of whom 290 were girls. Nevertheless, the idea was persistent, and it spread beyond Massachusetts. There were thirteen public normal schools in the country by 1860, including one maintained by the city of St. Louis.

After the Civil War, the movement developed more rapidly. The report of the United States Commissioner of Education for 1889–1890 showed 135 public normal schools, state and city, with 26,543 students in the teacher-training departments (some normals also

[1] Address of Governor Edward Everett at the dedication of the Barre Normal School, September 4, 1839.

offered high-school work for general students). Normal schools, however, did not acquire the monopoly in the training of grade-school teachers that has sometimes been assumed. High schools started teacher-training courses, such as that in Chicago in 1856. Also, during the nineteenth century, it was not necessary to go to any such schools in order to teach. It was sufficient in many states to pass such examinations as the local school authorities might prescribe.

Unfortunately, the normal schools suffered from some of the implications of their European antecedents. Whatever virtues the Prussian seminaries may have possessed, they were class institutions, designed for graduates of the folk schools, who would return to the folk schools as teachers. Teachers in the secondary schools of Prussia, on the other hand, were drawn from those who had attended such institutions and the university.

Although Massachusetts had no social classes such as those in Prussia, some of these connotations carried over nonetheless. College graduates became teachers in high schools and academies, tending to form a separate group and laying the groundwork for antagonisms and conflicts. The original entrance examinations for the Massachusetts state normals, while undoubtedly of high standard, demanded nothing more of the candidates than a common-school background. For many years, in Massachusetts and other states, graduates of elementary schools went directly to the normals, from which, after one-year or two-year courses, they were sent out to teach. Graduates of high schools who had taken a teacher-training course along the way tended, in consequence, to be regarded as a prestige group.

It was Massachusetts that took the first step to change the image of the normal schools. Under a new rule applied first in 1895, entrants to the normal schools of that state were required to be high-school graduates. The Massachusetts example was slowly followed. Eventually three-year and four-year courses, with high school graduation as prerequisite, were developed.

By the early 1920s, some major state universities were beginning to accept transfer credit from normal schools toward bachelor's degrees. As the normal schools in many states became transformed into teachers' colleges, they granted such degrees themselves. The development of teachers' colleges into state colleges produced institutions of general education that included programs for teacher education.

Horace Mann played no small part in the original founding of the first state normal schools of Massachusetts. This represented perhaps one of the most tangible outcomes of his period as secretary to the State Board. Along with this, he fostered another kind of institution, for which teachers may or may not remember him with gratitude, namely, the teachers' institute. These were devised for the continued education of teachers on the job. The idea had come from Henry Barnard, Horace Mann's counterpart in Connecticut, who had conducted one at Hartford in 1839. The first one in Massachusetts was held at Pittsfield in October, 1845, with none other than Horace Mann himself as the conductor.

Suggestions for Additional Reading

Borrowman, Merle. *The Liberal and the Technical in Teacher Education.* New York: Teachers College, Columbia University, 1956.

Cubberley, Ellwood P. (ed.). *Readings in Public Education in the United States.* Boston: Houghton Mifflin Company, 1934. Contains part of Governor Everett's address and other source documents on teacher training in the nineteenth century, pp. 317–349.

Hinsdale, B. A. *Horace Mann and the Common School Revival in the United States.* New York: Charles Scribner's Sons, 1898. Contains Governor Everett's address, pp. 157–158.

Dedication of the New Quincy School, Boston

New school buildings in Boston called for dedication ceremonies. So it was on June 26, 1848, when leading citizens gathered to dedicate the new building for the Quincy School. It was a kind of family affair, for the school was named after Josiah Quincy, an ex-mayor present at the dedication, while the mayor on hand to represent the city was his son, also named Josiah Quincy. Probably none of those present took more satisfaction in the dedication than the principal, John D. Philbrick, who had done much to bring it about.

This was more than the dedication of another school building. It was the heralding of a new kind of building and a new kind of school organization, representing a break with tradition and setting a pattern for the future. "This school house," said *The Boston Almanac* with pride in 1849, "being the last erected in the city, contains most of the modern improvements. . . . It is four stories high, and contains twelve school rooms, each of which accommodates 56 scholars, and a hall, furnished with settees, which will seat 700 pupils. It also has 6 small recitation rooms. Its greatest improvements consist in having a separate room for each teacher, and a separate desk for each scholar."[1]

Before that time even city schools had been organized along

[1] S. N. Dickinson, *The Boston Almanac* (Boston: B. B. Mussey & Co. and Thomas Groom, 1849), p. 80.

somewhat different lines. A city school building usually had a large room or hall for several hundred pupils, presided over by a master and his assistants. In Boston a building might have two such halls on separate floors, known respectively as the writing school and the grammar school, each with its own master. The pupils would spend a half day in each hall or school. This was known as the double-headed system. In Boston and in other cities there might also be small rooms called recitation rooms where the assistants could take groups of pupils, sometimes known as classes, for recitation and drill work.

Some modification of these arrangements had been under way before 1848, although no school system had placed teachers in separate rooms. There was no classification of pupils into groups that would stay together for a year's work. Those who favored a graded plan gained much support from Horace Mann's *Seventh Annual Report* (1843), in which he reported favorably on what he had seen in Prussia the year before.

"The first element of superiority in a Prussian school," wrote Mann, "and one whose influence extends throughout the whole subsequent course of instruction, consists in the proper classification of the scholars. In all places where the numbers are sufficiently large to allow it the children are divided according to ages and attainments, and a single teacher has charge only of a single class or of as small a number of classes as is practicable." Commenting on "the idleness and disorder that reign in so many of our schools, excepting where the debasing motive of fear puts the children in irons," Mann argued that "all these difficulties are at once avoided by a suitable classification."[2]

John D. Philbrick had become master of the Quincy School in 1847. A graduate of Dartmouth in 1842, Philbrick had been a high-school teacher and a writing master. He convinced the board of the need for a new building, one aimed at applying Horace Mann's ideas and his own. In the new building, the double-headed plan was abandoned. A single-headed school reigned in its place, with teach-

[2] *Seventh Annual Report,* 1843, p. 84.

ers in charge of their own groups. Philbrick left the school several years later and after some service in Connecticut returned to Boston as its superintendent in 1856.

Graded schools caught on and spread. The new plan became well established in city systems by the end of the 1860s. Children were now promoted, or held back, annually, moving along from one grade to the next. The familiar pattern of an eight-year elementary school and a four-year high school was in the making, and it became predominant in the post-Civil War era. There were, however, significant variations. Boston, along with most other school systems in Massachusetts and many in the rest of New England and in the state of New York, developed a nine-year elementary school. Kansas City, Missouri, settled for a seven-year school, and this became the pattern for a number of states in the South.

During the 1870s and 1880s, the pattern of elementary-school organization came under attack. Criticisms of presumed waste in the nine-year system of Massachusetts began to appear at least as early as 1873. In the late 1880s, President Charles W. Eliot of Harvard joined the critics, calling for a reduction of one year in the system and for the introduction of foreign languages, algebra, geometry, and physics in the seventh and eighth grades. Other criticisms were aimed at the idea of annual promotions. It was termed a lock-step system that retarded the progress of able pupils. The elementary schools of Cambridge, Massachusetts, in 1892 began to experiment with flexible promotions and a two-track system under which capable pupils could finish the nine-year course in seven years.

In 1899, the Committee on College Entrance Requirements of the National Educational Association recommended that the elementary-school program be cut to six years, with secondary education beginning in grade seven. This was a period of marked advocacy of various plans and systems, some of which called for separate schools for various combinations of the seventh, eighth, and ninth grades.

National attention was directed in 1910 to the adoption in Berkeley, California, of what were called introductory high schools, separate institutions for grades seven through nine. The idea spread quickly, as did also a new term for such institutions, namely, *junior high schools.* After 1915, there was furious advocacy of what had come to be known as the 6–3–3 plan.

All these plans, however, contained the basic assumption in the building of the Quincy School back in 1848 that students should be classified by grades or years. Within this assumption there could be much fluidity in the way grades were allotted to various institutions called elementary schools and junior and senior high schools. The early 1940s, however, witnessed the appearance of the ungraded primary plan, under which children were placed in a three-year block for the periods ordinarily represented by grades one through three, but without being so classified. These efforts did not gain much attention or publicity.

In the late 1950s a large volume of criticism, similar to that of the last decades of the nineteenth century, emerged against the system of annual promotions. The idea of separate grades was attacked as a system of shelves. Much of this appeared in a book entitled *The Nongraded Elementary School,* by John I. Goodlad and Robert H. Anderson. These views also affected secondary education, and B. Frank Brown in 1963 published *The Nongraded High School,* based on experimental work at the Melbourne, Florida, High School.

Meanwhile another dimension of Philbrick's plan was being widely modified, that of placing teachers with their own fixed groups in separate rooms of the same size. Under team teaching, groups of teachers share diversified functions with groups of pupils of various sizes in rooms designed for or adapted to large-group lectures or demonstrations, small-group discussions, and individual work.

Suggestions for Additional Reading

Brown, Bartley Frank. *The Nongraded High School.* Englewood Cliffs, N.J.: Prentice-Hall, Inc., 1963.

Cubberley, Ellwood P. (ed.). *Readings in Public Education in the United*

States. Boston: Houghton Mifflin Company, 1934. Contains documents on school organization and practices in city systems 1790–1857, pp. 280–288.

Goodlad, John I., and Robert H. Anderson. *The Nongraded Elementary School.* New York: Harcourt, Brace & World, 1959, 1963.

Shaplin, Judson T., and Henry F. Olds, Jr. (eds.). *Team Teaching.* New York: Harper & Row, 1964.

Massachusetts Law
on Compulsory Schooling

As LATE AS THE MIDPOINT of the nineteenth century, no state tried
to make parents send their children to school. Back in colonial times,
Massachusetts Bay had laid upon parents the obligation of seeing
that their children learned to read and had required communities
to supply teachers (see *1647*). A Massachusetts law in 1850 further
provided for the apprehension of children who were neither at school
nor at work. It was not until May 18, 1852, however, that the first
state law was enacted, inevitably in Massachusetts, for compulsory
school attendance.

"Every person," stipulated this law of 1852, "who shall have
any child under his control, between the ages of eight and fourteen
years, shall send such a child to some public school within the town
or city in which he resides, during at least twelve weeks, if the public
schools within that town or city shall be so long kept, in each and
every year during which such child shall be under his control, six
weeks of which shall be consecutive."[1] The penalty for not comply-
ing was a fine of $20.

Failure to send a child to the local public school was not considered a violation of the law if the child attended some school; if
he was "otherwise furnished with the means of education for a like

---

[1] Massachusetts, *General Laws,* 1852, chap. 240.

period of time"; or if he had "already acquired those branches of learning which are taught in common schools." These provisions left the parent free to send his child to a private school or to teach him at home. Similar provisions, expressed in various ways from state to state, exist in compulsory-attendance laws in our own times.

By 1890, twenty-seven states and territories had enacted compulsory-attendance laws. The next wave of such legislation culminated in the enactment of a compulsory-attendance law by Mississippi in 1918. This made it unanimous among the states. Unanimity was broken by the repeal of compulsory-attendance laws in South Carolina (1955), Mississippi (1956), and Virginia (1959).

Upper age limits of the laws in 1918 ranged from twelve to sixteen. These did not always mean what they said. In many of the states pupils were allowed to leave school at earlier ages if they had completed a stipulated number of grades. Nearly all the states gave work permits at earlier ages.

The effect of these exemptions was that only four states in 1918 substantially required full-time school attendance beyond fourteen years of age. By this time attendance in high schools had reached nearly the two-million mark, a phenomenon attributed by many to compulsory attendance. This interpretation may well be questioned in view of the qualifications made in the upper age limits.

In 1919, the National Education Association called for compulsory attendance to age eighteen, at least in part-time continuation schools (see *1917*). Utah had anticipated this resolution by enacting such a law earlier that year. After 1920 some advocacy developed of full-time compulsory attendance to age eighteen, but few such laws were passed. In 1960 there were only four states making this requirement; three others had moved their upper limit to age seventeen.

Compulsory-attendance laws were advocated for various reasons. Two were closely related, namely, the protection of the child's right to education and the campaign against child labor. Parents who kept their children out of school usually sent them to work.

Social workers and others concerned with child welfare accordingly have joined educators in support of compulsory attendance. The connection between compulsory attendance and child labor was emphasized in 1921 by a resolution of the National Child Labor Committee similar to the one passed by the National Education Association two years before.

Another argument for compulsory attendance has stressed the relationship between schooling and the welfare of society or the state. Some have gone so far as to recommend that all youth be required to spend a period of time in national civic service of an educational nature. Such a proposal was formally made by the National Education Association in 1919, calling upon the government of the United States to initiate and maintain the program and to direct it toward civic responsibility and vocational efficiency.

A by-product of the argument from state welfare has been the contention that only the public school can supply the desired civic training. On November 7, 1922, the people of Oregon passed a referendum by a vote of 106,996 to 93,349 requiring attendance at public schools through the eighth grade. The act was to take effect in 1926. Before that time, however, it was invalidated by the United States Supreme Court. "The fundamental theory of liberty upon which all governments in this Union repose," declared the court, "excludes any general power of the state to standardize its children by forcing them to accept instruction from public school teachers only."[2] This decision still stood in 1964, and no state could compel attendance at a public school.

Suggestions for Additional Reading

Fellman, David (ed.). *The Supreme Court and Education.* (Classics in Education No. 4.) New York: Bureau of Publications, Teachers College, Columbia University, 1962. Contains the text of the Pierce decision, pp. 1–3.

Goodman, Paul. *Compulsory Mis-Education.* New York: The Horizon Press, 1964.

[2] *Pierce, Governor of Oregon, et al.* v. *Society of Sisters of the Holy Names of Jesus and Mary,* 268 U.S. 510 (1925).

Organization of the
National Teachers' Association

IT WAS PROCLAIMED as a great occasion. The date was August 26, 1857, the place, Philadelphia. What happened was the founding of the National Teachers' Association. In spite of the greatness of the occasion, only forty-three people were on hand. This was, nonetheless, the birth of what later grew into the National Education Association, an organization with 943,581 members at the end of the school year of 1964–1965.

This was not the first organization of teachers. The call for the Philadelphia meeting had come from ten of the fifteen state associations already in existence. The first state association had been formed in Rhode Island on January 28, 1845, twelve years before.

Undaunted by the small beginning at Philadelphia, the newly-created Association met again the following year, this time at Cincinnati, and with Horace Mann as one of the speakers. After meeting at Washington, D.C. in 1859 and at Buffalo in 1860, the association suspended its national gatherings during the first two years of the Civil War, resuming them at Chicago in 1863. At Cleveland in 1870, it changed its name to the National Educational Association, which was subsequently clipped to National Education Association (hereafter referred to as the NEA) in 1908.

Membership remained small, as did also the attendance at the national conventions, until 1884. When Thomas W. Bicknell had been elected president of the Association in Saratoga Springs, New

York, the year before, only some 300 people had been on hand. An enterprising journalist of pedagogy and formerly State Commissioner of Schools in Rhode Island, Bicknell decided to change this state of affairs. After considering several sites for the 1884 convention, he and the other officers of the NEA made what appeared to be the strange choice of Madison, Wisconsin, then a city of only 12,000 people.

Bicknell organized a national campaign of publicity for the coming meeting. So successful was he that between 6,000 and 7,000 people (the numbers vary in the accounts) came to Madison for the convention, including 3,000 who were or who at this time became members of the NEA. Seven years later, Zalmon Richards, an old-time member who had presided at the Cincinnati meeting in 1858, proclaimed the convention of 1884 as the dawning of a new era for the association and its work.

It was in the late 1880s and in the 1890s that the NEA increased not only its membership, but its stature as a force in American educational thought and practice. Among the participants and leaders were President Charles W. Eliot of Harvard; William T. Harris, the United States Commissioner of Education; President James H. Baker of the University of Colorado and formerly principal of the Denver High School; and Nicholas Murray Butler, founder of Teachers College, Columbia University, and later president of Columbia. Under the leadership of these men and others, the NEA began to sponsor major projects, such as the Committee of Ten on Secondary-School Studies (see *1892*), a practice subsequently represented by its Commission on the Reorganization of Secondary Education (see *1918*), the Educational Policies Commission (1935), the Project on Instruction (1959), and other such projects.

After 1900, there was some feeling that the NEA had fallen under the domination of national leaders such as Eliot, Harris, and Butler. Protest against this alleged domination came, according to some interpreters, from classroom teachers and from women. In 1910, the Boston convention upset the recommendations of the Committee on Nominations and elected Ella Flagg Young, Chicago superintendent of schools, as president. The losers accused the winners of having used unethical, or at least undignified, tactics in the campaign. Wrangles continued after 1910; the old leaders, including Butler, gradually withdrew.

Much dissension was centered on the question of packing the various conventions with large numbers of temporary members from the local areas. Various experiments were conducted to eliminate this and the political maneuvers associated with it. In 1920, the association adopted the plan of transacting its official business through an assembly of delegates elected in the various state and local units.

The NEA continued to be a center of controversy. With its headquarters moved to Washington, D.C. in 1920, the NEA could keep in close touch with the United States Office of Education (see *1867*) and with Congress. This led to accusations of lobbying, with its defenders replying that no lobby, if that was the appropriate word, was devoted to a better cause. Some critics felt that the NEA concerned itself too much with the salaries and working conditions of teachers; others felt that it neglected the interests of classroom teachers and recommended membership in the American Federation of Teachers, an affiliate of the American Federation of Labor.

Although there were mixed feelings about the NEA as late as 1965, it remained in that year the only national organization dedicated to all aspects of education. It included teachers on all levels of the school, teachers of all subjects, and the great variety of administrative and supervisory workers and other school specialists. The controversy that continued in 1965 was perhaps an important sign of its active life.

Suggestions for Additional Reading

Cubberley, Ellwood P. (ed.). *Readings in Public Education in the United States.* Boston: Houghton Mifflin Company, 1934. Contains documents on the history of the NEA, pp. 504–510.

Wesley, Edgar B. *NEA: The First Hundred Years.* New York: Harper & Row, 1957.

The Land Grant College Act

ON JULY 2, 1862, President Lincoln signed the Land Grant College Act, making available to each state a grant of 30,000 acres for each senator and representative of that state in Congress. The grants were to be used for colleges in which the main aim was to teach subjects related to agriculture and the mechanic arts. Other scientific and classical studies, however, were not to be excluded. There was a specific provision in the law for including military science and tactics.

During the period following the adoption of the Constitution and through the 1820s, there had been much discussion of a national university for the United States. George Washington had left a bequest for such an institution. Succeeding presidents from John Adams through John Quincy Adams had given the idea their endorsement. While the Land Grant College Act of 1862 did not establish such a national university, it made the federal government a partner in the development of higher education throughout the states.

The main impulse for the act had come from advocates of the so-called practical studies. Much of this advocacy appeared in the writings of those who indulged themselves in what might be called the ideology or the statesmanship of education. This was the case with Jefferson, who in his plan for the University of Virginia had recommended not only technical and engineering subjects, but also manual training, the latter as a kind of extra-class activity. The higher technical studies represented a desire to advance the national welfare; manual training was viewed as a means of providing for what many regarded as a well-rounded education.

Inspiration for the manual-training or manual-labor idea came to American educators through the efforts of a Swiss nobleman, Philipp Emanuel von Fellenberg, who had maintained a famous school on his estate at Hofwyl in his own country. Ten such schools of manual labor, dedicated primarily to agriculture, appeared in the United States between 1821 and 1834. So appealing was the idea that the Pennsylvania legislature even recommended the manual arts in its controversial law of 1834, the one so eloquently defended by Thaddeus Stevens.

Both aspects of the practical studies—the national welfare and the well-rounded development of individuals—seemed to have natural appeal to philanthropists. One of these was Stephen Van Rensselaer of Troy, New York, who started a school of scientific agriculture in that city in 1824 and had it incorporated by the state a year later. Part of his purpose was to train teachers for school districts "belonging to the class of foreigners and mechanics." This institution, which the legislature had pronounced to be "highly beneficial to the public," eventually became the Rensselaer Polytechnic Institute, a famous college of engineering. The legislature also expressed its approval of "such individual efforts and such munificent application of the surplus wealth of individuals."

Although the movement for private manual-labor schools languished somewhat after the 1830s, a body of sentiment had been created for future development, especially along the lines of the higher and more technical kinds of practical studies. In 1854, the Illinois legislature voted a petition to the national Congress for land grants aimed at "the more liberal and practical education of our industrial classes and their teachers." This had been preceded by resolutions passed at a state convention of the Industrial League of Illinois, an organization sparked by the efforts of a professor at Illinois College named Jonathan B. Turner.

It was also in 1854 that Vermont sent to the national House of Representatives an antislavery Whig named Justin Smith Morrill. Three years later he introduced a bill along the lines of the Illinois petition. Passed by both houses of Congress in 1859, it was vetoed by President Buchanan. In his veto message, Buchanan expressed agreement with the aims of the bill, but feared that it would damage existing colleges where agriculture was taught as a science.

The next try, containing this time the additional provision for military tactics and raising the allotment from 20,000 to 30,000 acres per senator and representative, proved to be successful. Under this act of 1862, some 10,000,000 to 11,000,000 acres of land were made available to the states. It was followed by subsequent acts, differing from that of 1862 in their provisions but directed to the same purpose. Among these were the Experimental Stations Act of 1887, known as the Hatch Act, and the second Morrill Act, passed in 1890.

States used their grants from the law of 1862 in various ways. Eighteen of them added the study of agriculture and the mechanic arts to existing state institutions, while others founded new ones. A few granted portions of the funds to private colleges and universities. One instance of this was the arrangement made by the state of New York with Cornell University at Ithaca, a newly-founded institution which, like the Rensselaer Polytechnic Institute, had its origin in philanthropy, this time that of Ezra Cornell. Altogether, sixty-nine colleges and universities received funds under the Land Grant College Act.

As had been the case with the grants under the Ordinance of 1785, the states used their lands with varying degrees of financial wisdom. Some sold theirs fast and cheap in a market that was low at the time. Others managed to realize large amounts. In any case, the main impact of the act of 1862 appeared to be psychological, stimulating the states to new activity in higher education. Perhaps this new activity would have been inevitable in the industrial and commercial expansion of the nation after the Civil War.

Suggestions for Additional Reading

Cubberley, Ellwood P. (ed.). *Readings in Public Education in the United States.* Boston: Houghton Mifflin Company, 1934. Contains documents on the early movement for manual-labor schools, pp. 249–250 and 313–316.

Cubberley, Ellwood P., and E. C. Elliott. *State and County School Administration: Source Book.* New York: The Macmillan Company, 1915. Contains the Land Grant College Act of 1862 and related legislation, pp. 83–99.

United States Department (now Office) of Education

BEFORE 1867, the national government had no agency dealing with schools, although Congress had shown its awareness of education in relation to national policy. Nearly two years after the Civil War, on March 2, 1867, President Andrew Johnson signed a bill that established what was called a Department of Education. Initially proposed by the National Association of State and City School Superintendents, the bill had been introduced into the House of Representatives by James Garfield of Ohio on February 14, 1866, but had been delayed by lengthy debate in both houses.

The law established an office of Commissioner of Education, which, in spite of the term *department* used for the agency, was not to have cabinet status. The commissioner was to be appointed by the President of the United States, subject to confirmation by the Senate. He was to have a staff of three clerks. This was a modest undertaking indeed.

The purpose of the Department of Education, in the words of the law, was that of "collecting such statistics and facts as shall show the condition and progress of education in the several States and Territories, and of diffusing such information respecting the organization and management of schools and school systems, and methods of teaching, as shall aid the people of the United States in the establishment and maintenance of efficient school systems, and otherwise promote the cause of education throughout the country."[1]

President Johnson appointed Henry Barnard, at that time president of St. John's College, Annapolis, as the first commissioner. Before that time, Barnard had been successively Secretary of the Connecticut Board of Commissioners for Common Schools, State Superintendent of Schools in Rhode Island, State Superintendent of Education in Connecticut, and, very briefly, Chancellor of the University of Wisconsin. In Connecticut, his career had paralleled somewhat that of Horace Mann in Massachusetts. Barnard remained as commissioner until 1870, at which time he was succeeded by John Eaton.

After the agency had been in operation little over a year, occupying meanwhile two rooms in a rented building, its name was changed to the Office of Education, and it was placed in the Department of the Interior. In 1870, its name was changed to the Bureau of Education. Bureau it remained for fifty-nine years, becoming the Office of Education again in 1929. In 1939 it was transferred from the Department of the Interior to the Federal Security Agency. From there it was moved in 1953 to the newly-created cabinet Department of Health, Education, and Welfare.

The prestige of the office of commissioner has depended much on the incumbents. Since they had little power, the commissioners exerted influence largely through their personal reputations. There have been outstanding men in the office, but by almost universal agreement, the most celebrated of all was William Torrey Harris, who served from 1889 to 1906. A New Englander who had attended Yale, but without finishing the course for his degree, Harris gained his reputation as superintendent of the St. Louis, Missouri, public schools. He also acquired international distinction as a philosopher and some repute as a Dante scholar.

It was this period that constituted in some sectors of opinion the golden age of the NEA. Certainly it was the age in which Harris, Eliot, and Butler loomed large in NEA committees and reports.

[1] Quoted in Lloyd E. Blauch, "To Promote the Cause of Education," *School Life*, XXXV (May, 1953), 124.

Harris, particularly, was renowned as a platform warrior in the debates. Possibly his role in the NEA gave him a wider audience than his post as commissioner of education.

Up to 1887 the commissioners confined their activities largely to the collection of information and to its dissemination in thick annual reports. In that year, however, the bureau was given the function of administering schools and welfare services for Alaska. The reports continued, and some of their most engaging chapters were those dealing with the activities of the bureau with the Alaskan reindeer herds. In 1890 the bureau took on the responsibility of administering part of the second Morrill Act for land-grant colleges.

During the twentieth century, the bureau (after 1929, the office) was assigned various other administrative tasks, for example, in 1933, those pertaining to the Smith-Hughes program of vocational education, previously handled by an independent board (see *1917*). It became the administrative agency for the National Defense Education Act, passed in 1958 and expanded in 1964. Through all of this it remained an agency of information and research, functioning in part as a massive publishing house, including in its program two periodicals, *School Life* and *Higher Education*. These were merged in 1965 into a new one called *American Education*.

At the end of the First World War, the NEA began a strong drive to create a department of education with cabinet status. This was included in a series of bills beginning in 1919 with the Smith-Towner Bill. Representative Towner of Corning, Iowa, one of the sponsors of the bill, appropriately bore the given names of Horace Mann. These bills also contained provisions for general federal aid.

There was apparently strong national sentiment behind the drive for cabinet status. In 1921, presidents of thirteen other national organizations joined the president of the NEA in a petition to President Harding for the achievement of this goal. Among these were the presidents of the American Federation of Labor, the American Library Association, the Daughters of the American Revolution, the Women's Christian Temperance Union, the General Federation of Women's Clubs, and the Chairman of the Committee on Education of the Sunday School Council of Evangelical Denominations and the International Sunday School Association. In spite of all this support, the bills for cabinet status, including the provisions for federal aid, did not pass the Congress.

Finally, the goal of cabinet status was partly achieved through the creation of the Department of Health, Education, and Welfare. Through all of this the post of commissioner has remained, and it was held in 1965 by Francis Keppel, formerly dean of the School of Education at Harvard.

Suggestions for Additional Reading

Blauch, Lloyd E. "The Office of Education—Its Service and Staff," *School Life,* XXXII (April, 1950), 101, 112; (May, 1950), 119–127; (June, 1950), 140; XXXIII (October, 1950), 14; (December, 1950), 39.

Blauch, Lloyd E. "To Promote the Cause of Education," *School Life,* XXXV (May, 1953), 117–119 and 123–124; (June, 1953), 153–154. Contains the law establishing the Department of Education, with quotations from the debates in Congress.

Kursch, Harry. *The United States Office of Education: A Century of Service.* New York: Chilton Books, 1965.

Kalamazoo Decision

IN *Charles E. Stuart and Others* v. *School District No. 1 of the Village of Kalamazoo and Others,* the Supreme Court of Michigan on July 21, 1874, rendered a decision interpreted by many writers as giving powerful support to the development of public high schools. Stuart and his associates had challenged the right of the Kalamazoo district to collect taxes for the support of a high school and for the salary of a nonteaching superintendent of schools. The court upheld the district on both points.

The legal basis for high schools varied from state to state. Massachusetts required communities of given sizes to establish and maintain them. Some states authorized the establishment of individual high schools, as Pennsylvania had done for the Philadelphia Central High School in 1836. Others, such as New York in 1853, provided general authorization for high schools in the local units. In Michigan, a law passed in 1859 authorized school districts with more than 100 children to establish academic or high-school departments on the vote of the people in annual meeting. Over 100 high schools were established in Michigan before the Kalamazoo case.

Specifically, it was the complaint of the petitioners that even if they conceded the right of other districts to maintain high schools in which foreign and dead languages would be taught, the Kalamazoo district had never taken the vote required by the law for this purpose. Justice Thomas M. Cooley, who wrote the decision for the court, brushed this aside. There were, he said, many such irregularities in municipal administration. Moreover, the people of the district had substantially approved the high school by supporting it.

With this aspect of the complaint disposed of, Cooley turned to what he called the implied contention "that there is no authority in this state to make the high schools free by taxation levied on the people at large."[1] Michigan had a state university, established back in 1837. The logic of the complaint, declared Cooley, also raised the question of the competence of the state to supply this higher education at public expense.

"When this doctrine was broached to us," continued Cooley in the decision rendered by the court, "we must confess to no little surprise that the legislation and policy of our state were appealed to against the right of the state to furnish a liberal education to the youth of the state in schools brought within the reach of all classes. We supposed it had always been understood in this state that education, not merely in the rudiments, but in an enlarged sense, was regarded as an important practical advantage to be supplied at their option to rich and poor alike, and not as something pertaining merely to culture and accomplishment to be brought as such within the reach of those whose accumulated wealth enabled them to pay for it."

With the expression of these sentiments, reminiscent perhaps of Thaddeus Stevens' famous speech in the Pennsylvania legislature (see *1834*), Cooley proceeded to a review of school legislation in Michigan since its territorial days. The state constitution of 1850 had established free schools in local districts; from this, he argued, there was an "irresistible" inference that high schools would be provided "until every locality capable of supporting one was supplied."

Under this interpretation, high schools had been implied from the beginning. "If these facts," he concluded, "do not demonstrate clearly and conclusively a general state policy, beginning in 1817 and continuing until after the adoption of the present constitution, in the direction of free schools in which education, and at their op-

[1] *Charles E. Stuart and Others* v. *School District No. 1 of the Village of Kalamazoo and Others,* 30 Mich. 69 (1874).

tion the elements of a classical education, might be brought within the reach of all the children of the state, then, as it seems to us, nothing can demonstrate it."

Perhaps the most significant expression in the decision was the one including "the elements of a classical education." This made the high school part of a system of schools with continuity from the early grades through the university. It was still true in the 1870s that preparation for college involved the classical elements. Butts and Cremin have interpreted the decision, therefore, as a closing of the door against the possibility of a dual system,[2] such as may have been implied in Boston by the creation of a separate English High School (see *1827*), or the school system of Prussia. State Superintendent Pierce in Michigan had earlier contended for a system based on those of Prussia and New England. Apparently he had not intended to copy their dualistic features; at least Justice Cooley cited Pierce's contention without awareness that it may have conflicted with his decision.

The main impact of the Kalamazoo decision appeared to be that of establishing a climate of belief. Certainly Justice Cooley could not make his decision binding on other states. In 1878 an Illinois court in *Richards* v. *Raymond* followed suit by upholding the constitutionality of a law for the establishment of high schools by charter, as well as the right of a district to collect taxes for such schools, even though the course of study did not follow that prescribed by law. Two years later, the Illinois Supreme Court in *Powell et al.* v. *the Board of Education of School District No. 4, St. Clair County* upheld the right of the district to use public funds for the teaching of a foreign language, in this instance German.

Possibly the Kalamazoo decision encouraged legislatures in other states to go ahead with provisions for free high schools. Wisconsin did so in 1875, just one year after the decision. Minnesota followed in 1881. After long operating on the basis of authorizing individual high schools, Pennsylvania moved in 1887 to general authorization

[2] R. Freeman Butts and Lawrence A. Cremin, *A History of Education in American Culture* (New York: Henry Holt and Company, 1953), pp. 418–419.

in cities and in 1889 to such in all school districts. It may well be, however, that Justice Cooley in his famous decision was engaged not in creating, but rather in reflecting public opinion of his time.

Suggestions for Additional Reading

Cubberley, Ellwood P. (ed.). *Readings in Public Education in the United States*. Boston: Houghton Mifflin Company, 1934. Contains portions of the Kalamazoo decision, pp. 240–241.

Davis, Calvin O. *Public Secondary Education*. Chicago: Rand McNally & Company, 1917. A history of secondary education in Michigan.

Kandel, I. L. *History of Secondary Education*. Boston: Houghton Mifflin Company, 1930, pp. 432–449.

Committee of Ten on
Secondary School Studies

IF THE AMOUNT OF CONTROVERSY EVOKED be taken as a basis for judgment, the Committee of Ten on Secondary School Studies of the NEA was a successful venture indeed. Generated in the afternoon session of the association's National Council of Education at Saratoga Springs, New York, on July 9, 1892, the committee was officially approved by the Board of Directors three days later and given a $2,500 expense account for its work. Its chairman was the provocative and, to some, irritating fifty-eight-year-old president of Harvard University, Charles W. Eliot.

The Committee of Ten grew partly out of the desire of many high-school teachers and administrators for uniformity in college admission requirements. What they meant by this, however, was not a common group of subjects, but some consistency from one college to the next in what was covered in the entrance examinations for given subjects. Loud and varied were the complaints of schoolmen that the examinations in Greek, for example, covered different books from one college to the next.

There was yet another aspect to the impulse behind the Committee of Ten. This was the desire on the part of Eliot and other leaders, both in the colleges and in the secondary schools, to make the high school a broader channel to higher education. Under the prevailing pattern, it was the Classical Course, with its four years of Latin and two or three of Greek, that prepared high-school students for the entrance examinations of most recognized colleges. The English Course was regarded as terminal. True, one could go to college without going through secondary school at all, but this required private study in the classics. What the innovators sought was to make the subjects of the English Course acceptable for college entrance. As Eliot saw it, this demanded the strengthening of these subjects.

In its resolution of July 9, the National Council of Education directed the committee to arrange conferences of secondary-school and college people in the major subjects, these to recommend sequences of study good in themselves and acceptable to the colleges. By November, the Committee of Ten—consisting of five college presidents, two principals of public high schools, a college teacher, a headmaster of a private preparatory school, and Commissioner William T. Harris—had organized the conferences and appointed their members. The fields chosen for the conferences were Latin, Greek, mathematics, English, the other modern languages, natural history, physical science, geography, and one covering history, civil government, and political economy. Of these, only Latin, Greek, and mathematics were then regarded as college-preparatory subjects.

The conferences met simultaneously, but in different locations, in December, 1892. From their reports, Eliot and his nine associates drew up their general recommendations. In this process it was Eliot who took the lead. The other nine members disagreed with him and with one another on many points, and there was much revising of the general report. Nevertheless the writing of the report, although not in all respects its substance, was largely Eliot's work. In this he was aided closely by Principal John Tetlow of the Girls' High and Latin Schools of Boston, a fellow member of the committee. Eliot and Tetlow completed the final editing of the report in December, 1893. It was published with an 1893 dateline by the United States Bureau of Education, and 30,000 copies were sent throughout the country. The demand was so heavy that the report was soon re-printed by the American Book Company with an 1894 dateline and the addition of a topical index.

In the report appeared both the general recommendations of the committee and the specific outlines of subjects that had been prepared by the conferences. Each conference set forth what it felt should be taught in its field in the secondary school; some even rec-ommended sequences for the elementary grades. No distinctions were drawn in the teaching of these subjects so far as college-pre-paratory and terminal functions were concerned.

Against Eliot's preferences, the general report outlined four courses of study, namely, Classical, Latin-Scientific, Modern Lan-guage, and English. Eliot was inclined to favor free election by subjects. The four courses recommended were an expansion of the prevailing dualism between the Classical and English courses. Some schools already had them. The Classical Course set forth by the Committee of Ten, however, included more of the modern academic studies—English, history, and science—than was usually the case at that time. Their English Course, unlike many then in existence, required one foreign language, ancient or modern. English, mathe-matics, and history were common to all four of the committee's courses, but in varying amounts.

With regard to the ancient languages, the committee's Classical Course required both Latin and Greek. The latter was reduced to two years from the prevailing three-year stipulation. The Latin-Scientific course was a compromise that required Latin, but no Greek. Neither Latin nor Greek was required in the Modern Lan-guage and in the English Course.

As general policy, the committee took the position that second-ary schools existed primarily to prepare for life, with college prepa-ration as only an incidental object. It recognized the fact that only a small proportion of the secondary-school graduates in that period went to college. On the other hand, it insisted that every graduate who wished to go to college might do so. It recommended that col-leges accept students who completed any one of the four courses outlined in the report. This meant accepting some who had taken neither Latin nor Greek. With this Eliot fully concurred.

The storm of controversy about the report broke out at once, appearing first in a two-day discussion at the February, 1894, meeting of the Department of Superintendence of the NEA. It raged throughout the spring in pedagogical journals throughout the country and in a number of regional and state meetings of educational associations. When the report was officially submitted by the committee to its parent body, the National Council, at the summer NEA meeting at Asbury Park, New Jersey, another bitter discussion took place. The committee was discharged at Eliot's request, but the controversy went on.

Most of the discussion ran against the report, but for a variety of reasons. The classicists felt that it disparaged the place of Latin and Greek. In particular, the American Philological Association attacked it because of the proposed reduction of the amount of Greek in the Classical Course. Those who wanted a larger place for manual training and the business subjects deplored the fact that no conferences had been arranged for these and that they did not appear in the recommended courses of study.

Some resented the presence of the five college presidents on the committee and denounced the report as college domination of the secondary schools. Others wanted to retain the traditional distinction between preparatory and terminal programs. City superintendents, many of whom had come to their posts through elementary-school teaching, objected to the discussion of the elementary-school curriculum in some of the conference recommendations.

Probably a major element in the controversy was President Eliot himself. He had ruffled many feathers in his critical speeches, and he was now attacked as a college president trying to interfere with the public schools. For the most part he blandly disregarded the attacks. On several occasions, however, he responded sharply to some of the criticisms, particularly those made by G. Stanley Hall, President of Clark University.

Just what direct influence the report had is difficult to say.

Certainly the volume of discussion it evoked set a climate favorable to change. College admission requirements did become more flexible, and more students found it possible to gain higher education without Latin or Greek. The creation of the College Entrance Examination Board (see *1900*) was fully consistent with the spirit of the report, especially the desire for uniformity within subjects.

One result of the Committee of Ten was a vogue for national committees on educational questions, many of these sponsored by the NEA. In 1895, the NEA appointed a Committee on College Entrance Requirements, largely as a follow-up to the work of the Committee of Ten. With Augustus F. Nightingale, Assistant Superintendent of Schools in Chicago, as its chairman, this committee in its report of 1899 fully endorsed the position of the Committee of Ten with respect to the unity of the terminal and preparatory functions. It moved toward Eliot's position by recommending the abandonment of set courses of study and their replacement by a system of constants and free electives. Surprisingly, this report was calmly accepted, although not necessarily followed, while controversy was still raging about the Committee of Ten.

In the years after 1900, the storms died away, but the image of the Committee of Ten as an agency of college domination tended to persist. As folklore about it developed, the committee was understood to have advocated the reverse of what it did advocate. Through all of this, one consolation remained that might have pleased Eliot and his nine associates. As late as 1965, seven decades after its tumultuous appearance, the report was still being debated and discussed.

Suggestions for Additional Reading

Krug, Edward A. (ed.). *Charles W. Eliot and Popular Education.* (Classics in Education No. 8.) New York: Bureau of Publications, Teachers College, Columbia University, 1961. Contains portions of the report of the Committee of Ten, pp. 83–99, plus various addresses and articles by Eliot in that period.

Krug, Edward A. *The Shaping of the American High School*. New York: Harper & Row, 1964. Chaps. I–IV.

Latimer, John Francis. *What's Happened to Our High Schools*. Washington, D.C.: Public Affairs Press, 1958. A modern defense of the Committee of Ten.

Wesley, Edgar B. *NEA: The First Hundred Years*. New York: Harper & Row, 1957. Contains a modern criticism of the Committee of Ten, pp. 71–75.

★ ★ ★ ★ ★ 1900 ★ ★ ★ ★ ★

College Entrance Examination Board

THE ESTABLISHMENT ON NOVEMBER 17, 1900, of the College Entrance Examination Board provided an instrument for uniformity in college entrance examinations. President Eliot had long been recommending such a board, but the main work of bringing it into existence was done by Nicholas Murray Butler, who became president of Columbia University in 1901.

Butler's vehicle for the creation of the board was the Association of College and Preparatory Schools of the Middle States and Maryland, an organization formed in 1892. It was to the 1899 convention of this group, held in December at the State Normal School of Trenton, New Jersey, that Butler brought his specific proposal. Vigorous discussion took place, with fears expressed by some of the college presidents, especially F. L. Patton of Princeton and Ethelbert Warfield of Lafayette, that colleges might lose the freedom of selecting their own students.

Eliot was present as a guest of the association and warmly supported Butler's proposal. According to one version of the proceedings, he gravely assured President Warfield that Lafayette College under this plan could even decide to admit only those applicants who failed the examinations. The roar of laughter following this observation, said Butler later, had much to do with the acceptance of the proposal itself.[1] In any case, the association did pass a resolution for the creation of such a board.

With this behind him, Butler, as chairman of a committee organized for this purpose, called the meeting in New York City at which the board was formally established. Present at this meeting on November 17, 1900, were representatives of eleven colleges and universities and five representatives of secondary schools.

The first examinations were conducted during the week of June 17, 1901, at 67 centers in the United States and two in Europe. They were taken by 973 students, of whom more than half were planning to enter Columbia University or its affiliate, Barnard College. On this occasion, examinations were given in English, Latin, Greek, German, French, mathematics, history, chemistry, and physics. They were prepared by committees, each of which included two college representatives and one representative of secondary schools. Specific definitions of the subjects, however, did not necessarily follow those in the conference reports of the Committee of Ten. By this time new definitions were available from various scholarly groups, such as the American Historical Association and the American Philological Association, some of which had worked closely with the NEA Committee on College Entrance Requirements of 1895–1899.

What the examinations did was to test the achievement of students in subjects demanded by the colleges to which entrance was sought. The board set no pattern of subjects for college entrance, and it made no stipulations for graduation from high schools. It was this feature of the board that delighted Eliot. Under its auspices, no student had to take any particular subject, such as Latin, and no college had to require it. If a college did require it, the board stood ready to test achievement in it.

Apparently things went smoothly at these first examinations,

---

[1] Nicholas Murray Butler, *Across the Busy Years* (New York: Charles Scribner's Sons, 1939), I, 199–200.

although one of the founders of the board said later that the examination in chemistry had been a disaster. Perhaps he referred to the fact that of 190 students who took this examination, 120 received marks of less than 60 on the basis of 100. This disaster did not block the continued work of the board, for the following year 1,362 students appeared. On this second round of examinations, the board expanded its list of subjects to include Spanish, botany, geography, and drawing.

In the period following 1902, the system of admitting to college by means of examinations came into disfavor in many parts of the country. Most colleges began to admit by certificate or diploma from accredited schools (see *1901*); some had been doing so at least as far back as the 1870s. For those colleges still using the examination system, the board provided a valuable service. Even Harvard, which had remained aloof in spite of Eliot's devotion to the board, came over to a complete use of the system by 1917.

This was also a period of greatly increased college attendance. Even though the work of the board applied only to a small proportion of those seeking college admission, the absolute number taking the examinations ran into the thousands. In 1925, a quarter of a century after it was established, the board administered its examinations to 19,775 candidates in 316 centers. These came from 1,691 secondary schools, about equally divided between public and private institutions. It was estimated in that year that the examinations were taken by about 5 percent of those who entered college.

Over the course of years, many changes took place in the nature and work of the board. In 1942, it went over largely to the use of so-called new type or objective tests. The board itself was reorganized in 1948, and the administration of the testing program was assigned to a new agency, the Educational Testing Service of Princeton, New Jersey. An additional function assumed by the board was that of guidance to prospective college students; in this connection it has published a *College Handbook*. In 1954, the board began a testing program for advanced placement, under which it became possible for students to gain college credit for work done in high school. The role of the board in curriculum planning was symbolized by the creation of its Commission on Mathematics in 1955 and its Commission on English in 1959.

After the Second World War, a great increase took place in the number of member colleges, the figure rising to 253 in 1956 and 543 in 1963. In 1959 it began providing memberships for secondary schools as well; by 1963 there were 204 such members. For colleges, membership meant the regular and substantial use of at least one program of the board's tests. There was great flexibility in the use of the various testing programs, some colleges requiring aptitude tests only (the board had started giving these in 1926), others requiring achievement tests only for scholarship applicants or for those seeking advanced placement, and still others requiring achievement tests in three subjects, the maximum number allowed by the board.

Like the NEA and other groups, the board acquired critics as well as friends. Its testing program was accused of stimulating coaching in the secondary schools. The board itself always advised against coaching and insisted that the best way to anticipate the examinations was to teach good courses. It was not always easy, however, to gain agreement along these lines. The examinations obviously reflected the views of the board, particularly the views of the examining committees in the various subjects. The board was accused, therefore, of dominating the secondary schools and of discouraging experimentation with new content and method.

The latter point was made again in 1958, when students who had taken the so-called new physics of the Physical Science Study Committee did less well on the College Board's physics test than might have been expected. Defenders of the Physical Science Study Committee charged that the conventional tests were inappropriate for those who had taken the new physics. The board, however, showed itself willing to cooperate with this experimental venture, preparing a special test for the new physics and moving in 1962 to a new combined test designed to be appropriate for both groups.

Suggestions for Additional Reading

College Entrance Examination Board. *The Work of the College Entrance Examination Board 1901–1925*. Boston: Ginn and Company, 1926.

College Entrance Examination Board. *The College Board Today*. Princeton, New Jersey: The Board, 1963.

Fuess, Claude M. *The College Board: Its First Fifty Years*. New York: Columbia University Press, 1950.

Commission on Accredited
Schools of the
North Central Association

Assembled in the Auditorium Hotel of Chicago on March 30, 1901, the delegates to the convention of the North Central Association of Colleges and Secondary Schools voted to establish a new commission, called the Commisison on Accredited Schools. Its purpose was to draw up a list of secondary schools that met defined standards and whose graduates could be accepted by colleges without examinations. This action provided formal organization for what was known as the Western system of college admission by diploma or certificate, as contrasted with the so-called Eastern system of admission by examination, symbolized the year before by the creation of the College Entrance Examination Board.

The North Central Association had come into existence in 1895 as an outgrowth of the Michigan Schoolmasters' Club. As its title stated, it was a regional association, much like the New England Association of Colleges and Preparatory Schools, founded in 1885, and the Association of Colleges and Preparatory Schools of the Middle States and Maryland, founded in 1892. With the creation of the North Central Association and of the Association of Colleges and Preparatory Schools of the Southern States in 1895, most of the country was covered. North Central extended over the largest range of geography, including Colorado to the west and Ohio to the east.

It was after six years of existence that North Central decided not only to be an instrument for study and discussion, but to strike out in what would be, for such associations, the new direction of accreditation. There was, however, ample precedent for such a move. Many colleges had long been admitting students on certificate. For the most part this had been a haphazard arrangement, but the University of Michigan since 1869–1870 had been conducting its program along systematic lines.

In the Michigan plan, faculty members visited secondary schools to evaluate the preparation of the teachers, the program of studies, provisions for libraries and laboratories, and the teaching itself. The University of Wisconsin and the University of Illinois followed with similar plans. In other states, such as Indiana and Minnesota, accreditation was conducted by state departments of public instruction. The action of North Central in creating its Commission on Accredited Schools was intended not to displace the existing arrangements, but to bring them together in a coordinated system.

Acting on the recommendations of its commission, the association in 1902 created a Board of Inspectors and adopted standards for accreditation. These included an inventory of subjects to be offered, the stipulation that the teachers be college graduates, and a statement of minimum requirements for graduation. The latter were stated as fifteen units, a unit consisting of a year's work of at least 35 weeks in a class meeting four or five times weekly in periods of 45 minutes each. The association rejected a proposal from the commission that only schools with at least five teachers be accredited. In 1904, the commission recommended and obtained the accreditation of 156 schools, public and private.

The commission did not confine its attention to secondary schools. During this period efforts were being extended in the North Central Association, as well as in other groups, to define the high school as a four-year institution. One of the major barriers to this was the tendency of many colleges to accept students who had less than a four-year preparatory course. This made the colleges, particularly in the South, competitors with high schools for available students. In 1904, the North Central Association, acting on the recommendation of the Commission on Accredited Schools, voted to deny membership to colleges requiring less than fifteen units for admission.

Two years later, in 1906, the Carnegie Foundation for the Advancement of Teaching adopted a similar policy, but with only fourteen units, in defining colleges eligible to participate in its pension plan. Although the term *unit* was later referred to as *Carnegie unit,* it was invented neither by North Central nor by the Carnegie Foundation. It had come from the 1899 report of the NEA Committee on College Entrance Requirements. A common national definition of the term was recommended in 1909 by a conference representing the four regional associations.

The name of the commission was changed in 1906 to the Commission on Accreditation of Schools and Colleges, and the Association began formal accreditation of colleges in 1912. The first list of accredited colleges and universities contained the names of seventy institutions. College accreditation was used mainly in the granting of transfer credits. In 1916, the commission was divided into two, one for secondary schools and one for colleges.

Advocates of the diploma system pursued their cause with ideological zeal. Speech after speech was made celebrating the contrast between this, sometimes referred to as the organic system, with the work of the College Entrance Examination Board, referred to in North Central discussions as the feudal system. North Central, like the other regional associations, had a representative on the College Board; in 1918, however, it decided to sever this relationship with a system of which it disapproved. The missionary efforts of North Central first met with success in 1913, when the Southern Association began accreditation. The Middle States Association adopted the idea in 1928, and the New England Association began accrediting colleges and secondary schools in 1953. In 1917, the Northwest

Association was formed, and it began accreditation the following year. The Western Association has been engaged in accreditation since its formation in 1962.

Meanwhile, North Central continued to grow, both in numbers and influence. In 1915, it had 1,060 secondary schools and 122 colleges and universities as institutional members; membership and accreditation were by then synonymous, the two categories having been combined in 1912. The influence of the association was informal, but powerful. As a purely voluntary agency, the association was in no way an instrument of official control. Still, the desire for accreditation was so strong that the unofficial influence of the association often counted more than the actions of legislatures or the rulings of state departments of public instruction. Administrators and faculties of local schools awaited the visits of the North Central inspectors with fear and trembling indeed.

At no time was it the case that graduates of nonaccredited schools were absolutely denied admission to the member colleges without taking examinations. Colleges and universities under North Central, as under the College Board, made their own decisions about whom to admit. Neither was it the case that any graduate of an accredited school could go to any college merely on the strength of his diploma. He still had to meet the specific requirements of the college he wished to attend. The impact of the system was tangible enough, but it was partly symbolic as well.

The association frequently became concerned about the possibility that its police function, as it was called, might swallow its other activities. Accordingly, it sponsored studies of the secondary-school curriculum and sought to encourage creative experimentation. In 1933, its Commission on Unit Courses and Curricula published a summary report, *High School Curriculum Reorganization,* of the activities it had been carrying on since 1916. Association leaders sought increasingly to expand the positive functions of the organization and to handle accreditation in a manner consistent with experimentation in local schools.

In 1957, the association aroused the ire of the press and some other observers by dropping the Holland Christian High School of Holland, Michigan, from its accredited list. The reason for this action was the refusal of this school to include so-called practical subjects, homemaking and industrial arts, in its curriculum. On this occasion, however, the uproar was directed not against the accrediting function as such, but against the supposed desire of the association to uphold what the critics regarded as an antiacademic point of view.

In 1964, the association, expanded by then to a membership of 3,692 secondary schools, was following policies that represented a blend of the old and the new. Schools once admitted were to retain membership for an indefinite period and would be checked only through annual reports submitted by their staffs. Specific criteria were stated for judging the preparation of teachers, the teaching load, libraries, instructional equipment, school plant, supervisory services, and programs of studies.

With regard to programs of studies, schools were called upon to provide instruction in eight fields, namely, language arts, science, mathematics, social studies, foreign languages, fine arts, practical arts, and health and physical education. Under strict application of this list, a school might be denied membership for lacking one or more of the stipulated fields. Those who favored the so-called academic studies might have applauded when such denial was based on the lack of foreign languages; others might have applauded with equal vigor when the denial was based on the lack of the practical arts.

Suggestions for Additional Reading

Davis, Calvin O. *A History of the North Central Association of Colleges and Secondary Schools 1895–1945*. Ann Arbor, Michigan: The Association, 1945.

Krug, Edward A. *The Shaping of the American High School*. New York: Harper & Row, 1964. Chaps. VI–VII.

North Central Association of Colleges and Secondary Schools. *Policies and Criteria for the Approval of Secondary Schools 1963–64*. Chicago: The Association, 1964.

The Smith-Hughes
Act for Vocational Education
(with the Vocational Education
Act of 1963)

MEMBERS OF THE National Society for the Promotion of Indus-trial Education, gathered around the banquet tables of their Phila-delphia convention on February 23, 1917, were listening to speeches and waiting for news from Washington. When it came, the toast-master stopped the speaker and announced that President Wilson had signed the Act for Vocational Education, popularly known as the Smith-Hughes Act. According to the report on this session, the news ended all the speeches for the night. Presumably even the speaker who had been interrupted joined the festivities. A major goal of the society had been achieved.

The Smith-Hughes Act was not only a victory for the society, but also the culmination of an impulse that had started far back in American educational history. Among the antecedents of the act were the private manual-labor schools of the 1820s, the individual bequests of philanthropists such as Stephen Van Rensselaer, the actions of state legislatures such as that of Pennsylvania in 1834, and the passing of the Land Grant College Act of 1862.

After the Civil War, the campaign for agricultural and industrial education took on new vigor, stimulated particularly by the exhibit of the Russian Imperial Technical Schools at the Philadelphia Exposition of 1876. By 1900, manual training was a subject in many elementary schools, and a new kind of high school, known as the manual-training high school, had appeared as well.

Two events in 1906 set off the immediate campaign that led to the Smith-Hughes Act. One was the report of the Massachusetts Commission on Technical and Industrial Education, known as the Douglas Report from the name of the governor who had appointed the commission. This report, dramatizing the alleged need for vocational education, was widely circulated throughout the country. The other was the founding on November 16, 1906, of the National Society for the Promotion of Industrial Education, a group made up of educators, social workers, manufacturers, and civic leaders.

Where the act of 1862 had provided for technical education in the colleges, the new campaign sought to introduce its counterpart in the public schools. Among the arguments set forth were the supposed decline of apprenticeship, the presence of many pupils who allegedly had neither interest in nor talent for the academic program, the need for trained workers to keep the United States abreast of other industrial nations such as Great Britain and Germany, and the need for economic growth. The campaign was widely supported, although some critics were suspicious about the presence in it of such groups as the National Association of Manufacturers. Even organized labor, initially skeptical, came through with a qualified endorsement of it in the American Federation of Labor Convention of 1910.

Educators were enthusiastic for the campaign in its early stages. The NEA from 1907 to 1909 devoted many of its sessions to oratory and exhortation for the cause. After 1909 some rifts began to appear. Many educators were alienated by the tendency of the society and others associated with the new movement to disparage what had been done in manual training. Others feared the development of what were known as trade schools, detached from the regular elementary and secondary school system. The unsuccessful attempt in Massachusetts, 1907–1909, and the successful attempt in Wisconsin, 1911, to set up separate boards of control for vocational schools, drove educators to a feeling that vocational education had to be kept within bounds. On one point the general educators and the vocational enthusiasts agreed, namely, the development of continuation or part-time schools for those who left school early. This device came from Germany and was first introduced to the American scene in Cincinnati in 1909.

Undaunted by the defection of some of the general educators, the society defined and pressed on to its major goal, the passing of national financial aid to the states for vocational education. Acting with congressional authorization, President Wilson early in 1914 appointed a Commission on National Aid to Vocational Education, a group that produced a 500-page report in less than sixty days. As was expected, the commission recommended national aid.

The Smith-Hughes Bill was introduced in the lame-duck session of 1914, but no action was taken. It was reintroduced with some modifications in 1915. After that it was delayed by oratory and by difficulties involved in smoothing out the amendments passed in the two houses. President Wilson made appeal for the bill on the grounds of national defense. Finally, the joint conference committee had the bill ready for the presidential signature. By this time, the members of the Society for the Promotion of Industrial Education were impatient and apprehensive. It is little wonder that they exploded with joy when word arrived on February 23, 1917, that Wilson had signed the bill.

The act established a Federal Board for Vocational Education, consisting of the secretary of agriculture, the secretary of commerce, the secretary of labor, the commissioner of education, and three others, these to be appointed by the President with Senate confirmation. This board was to administer the granting of the funds to the states and to set up programs of studies and reports.

A sum of $1,500,000 was designated for aid to the states during the first year. This was to increase to a maximum of $7,000,000 a year by 1926 and to remain at that level. The money was to be used to train and pay the salaries of teachers, supervisors, and directors of agriculture, home economics, and trade and industrial subjects. All funds were to be matched by the states.

To get the money, it was necessary for a state to create a vocational board. This could be the regular state board of public instruction. In this way, the act referred to the states the still troublesome issue of dual control. Beyond this, a state was obligated to submit plans covering schools and equipment, courses of study, methods of instruction, and the qualifications of teachers. It was stipulated in the act that the work had to be done in public schools of less than college grade and for the purpose of fitting students for useful employment.

By January 1, 1918, all the states had submitted plans, and the system was ready to go into effect. Some educators were critical of the act for leaving the door open to dual control. Others feared the possibility of federal control of state and local programs. Nevertheless, the Smith-Hughes program rapidly became a going concern. It did not, however, produce the great upsurge in vocational education that had been expected. Enrollments in programs covered by the act did increase throughout the 1920s and again after 1934 until the entry of the United States in the Second World War, this being followed by a new period of increase beginning in 1945.

Some of the specific provisions of the Smith-Hughes Act were supplemented by new laws, beginning with the George-Reed Act of 1929 and including the George-Deen Act of 1934 and the George-Barden Act of 1946. The George-Deen Act added a fourth field, that of distributive education, moving thereby beyond training for direct production and into the realm of service employment. Eleven more acts dealing with specific circumstances in vocational education were passed between 1947 and 1961.

The signing of the Vocational Education Act of 1963 by Lyndon B. Johnson on December 18 of that year constituted a reorientation for the future of the broad program of vocational education in American schools. This law authorized a permanent program of funds to the states, beginning with $60,000,000 for the year ending June 30, 1964, and increasing to $225,000,000 a year in 1967 and thereafter. After the first year the funds were to be matched by the states. All the federal funds under this legislation were to be granted in addition to those from the Smith-Hughes and George-Barden acts.

Based on recommendations made by a twenty-five-member panel of consultants to the Department of Health, Education, and Welfare, the Vocational Education Act of 1963 included virtually all occupations except those demanding professional training and college degrees. Listed as groups eligible for training under its provisions were those in high school, those who had completed or left high school, those at work seeking advanced training or retraining, and those with academic or other handicaps. Construction of new buildings was also authorized under the act. Of great importance was the provision of funds for research programs designed to keep vocational training up-to-date and to anticipate and provide for technological change. Under a supplementary feature of the act, temporary funds, covering a four-year period, were made available for a work-study program of part-time employment for youth.

In his comments made at the signing of this act, President Johnson referred to it as dramatic evidence of our commitment "to education as the key to our social and economic and technological and moral progress."[1] With these sentiments, the members of the National Society for the Promotion of Industrial Education would have fully concurred.

Suggestions for Additional Reading

Hawkins, Layton S., Charles A. Prosser, and John C. Wright. *Development of Vocational Education*. Chicago: American Technological Society, 1951. Contains the text of the Smith-Hughes Act of 1917, pp. 597–604.

[1] "Remarks of the President upon the Signing of H.R. 4955, The Vocational Education Act of 1963, in the Cabinet Room, December 18, 1963," *Selected Education Acts of 1963* (Washington, D.C.: U.S. Government Printing Office, 1963), p. 89.

Keppel, Francis. "Vocational Education: A Program for Tomorrow," *American Vocational Journal,* XXXIX (February, 1964), pp. 15–18.

Krug, Edward A. *The Shaping of the American High School.* New York: Harper & Row, 1964. Chap. X.

Selected Education Acts of 1963. Washington, D.C.: U.S. Government Printing Office, 1963. Contains the text of the Vocational Education Act of 1963, pp. 91–100, and of the comments made by President Lyndon B. Johnson on the signing of the bill, p. 89.

"The Vocational Education Act of 1963," *School Life,* XLVI (March–April, 1964), pp. 3–12. Contains detailed analysis of the Vocational Education Act of 1963, with portions of the text.

Commission on the Reorganization of Secondary Education

DURING THE FINAL YEAR of the First World War, the United States Bureau of Education published a 32-page pamphlet, drab in appearance but not in content, that established for at least three decades the major dimensions of discussion about secondary schools. This pamphlet, called *Cardinal Principles of Secondary Education,* was the product of the Commission on the Reorganization of Secondary Education, appointed by the NEA back in 1913. More specifically, it was the product of the imagination and determination of the commission's chairman, Clarence Kingsley, onetime teacher of mathematics in the Manual Training High School of Brooklyn, New York.

A graduate of Colgate University, Kingsley had taught mathematics at that institution before taking his master's degree at Teachers College, Columbia University, and going from there in 1904 to his job in Brooklyn. This was the second great decade of increasing enrollments in public high schools, the total number of students going from a half million in 1900 to nearly a million in 1910. It was also the period of the campaign for vocational education and for a popular doctrine known as education for social efficiency.

Active discussion of these and related matters was taking place in the High School Teachers' Association of New York City. Kingsley joined and soon assumed leadership in this group, playing a major role in a report on the articulation between high school and college, with the prophetic subtitle, "The Reorganization of Secondary Education."

Kingsley took copies of this report with him to the Department of Secondary Education at the Boston NEA convention of 1910. The department promptly created a committee called The Committee on the Articulation of High School and College, consisting of national leaders in secondary education, with Kingsley as chairman. The following year at San Francisco, Kingsley was ready with the report. Both for graduation from high school and for admission to college, the report recommended a program in English, social studies, and natural science, with an option for the student of taking either foreign languages or mathematics. Included was provision for a free margin of four units that might be used for any subjects taught in the high school, such as vocational subjects.

Equipped with a set of subcommittees for working on the various instructional fields, the committee was expanded by the NEA in 1913 into the Commission on the Reorganization of Secondary Education. Kingsley, who had left New York the year before to become a state inspector of high schools in Massachusetts, became chairman of the new enterprise. As such, he served also as chairman of the central reviewing committee that began under his leadership to work on a general report.

The responsibility for a general report on secondary education was no light one. Confronting the reviewing committee were several critical issues. One of these was the place of vocational education, particularly whether it should be carried. on in special schools or in the general high schools. Closely related to this was the question of differentiation, that is, the practice of separating students into defined groups with courses of study labeled academic, vocational, commercial, and the like.

Some advocates of differentiation wanted it extended downward to begin in the seventh grade, a point of view stimulated by the appearance of the separate junior high school as an institution for grades seven through nine. The Department of Superintendence gave its endorsement to such early differentiation. Also present in the climate of the times was the idea that the right of any subject to exist in the high-school program should be judged by its proved contribution to the aim of social efficiency.

The reviewing committee worked on the general report for nearly three years. As its record shows, it was Kingsley who prepared the drafts for discussion, who took the lead in revising the drafts, and who held the members to their common task through frequent and lengthy meetings. Like Eliot with the Committee of Ten, Kingsley did not always carry his points. Still, the writing of the final document was largely his.

Beginning with an overview of social and pedagogical changes presumably requiring a new examination of secondary education, the report called for democratic education of benefit both to the individual and society. It stated seven aims of education, namely, health, command of fundamental processes, worthy home membership, vocation, citizenship, worthy use of leisure, and ethical character.

With these aims, the report placed vocational education in the larger context of the pedagogical enterprise as a whole. Beyond this, the aims constituted perhaps a somewhat humanized version of social efficiency. The report challenged teachers in all subjects, academic and practical, to relate their work more closely to these aims. This may have been an unfortunate recommendation, but it was a more moderate expression of the temper of the times than many being voiced in journals and in meetings of the NEA.

On school organization, the report advised against special vocational schools and called for a comprehensive high school that would include a variety of programs. It endorsed differentiation, but not for the seventh and eighth grades. The idea of constants or common subjects was recommended, but the report did not say what these should be. It was implied, however, that English and social studies should be well represented. With regard to college admission, the report continued the tradition of the Committee of Ten by recommending that all high-school graduates be accepted.

Perhaps the most striking recommendation in the report was the one that called for universal secondary schooling. All normal boys and girls, said the report, should be encouraged to stay in school until eighteen years of age, and if possible, with full-time attendance. It recommended at least part-time compulsory schooling to age eighteen, but insisted this should take place in the comprehensive high school, not in continuation schools.

The report was favorably received. It evoked practically no controversial discussion. Development of secondary education followed its general lines. Comprehensive high schools prevailed over special vocational schools for the most part. Differentiation did not survive in the seventh and eighth grades. The idea that all youth should go to high school became widespread in American life.

It was the statement of the seven aims that seemed most to capture the imagination of the pedagogical world. The term *cardinal principles* had referred to the whole report, but the seven aims themselves became known popularly as the seven cardinal principles. Generations of prospective teachers memorized these aims and wrote them down on tests. Practically all statements of aims that appeared as late as the 1950s sustained the ideology of those in the report.

Suggestions for Additional Reading

Commission on the Reorganization of Secondary Education. *Cardinal Principles of Secondary Education.* Washington, D.C.: United States Bureau of Education Bulletin No. 35, 1918.

Cremin, Lawrence A. "The Problem of Curriculum Making: An Historical Perspective." *What Shall the High Schools Teach?* 1956 Yearbook of the Association for Supervision and Curriculum Development. Washington, D.C.: The Association, 1956. Chap. I.

Krug, Edward A. *The Shaping of the American High School.* New York: Harper & Row, 1964. Chap. XV.

★ ★ ★ ★ ★ 1919 ★ ★ ★ ★ ★

Progressive Education Association

THE NEWLY-FORMED Association for the Advancement of Progressive Education held its first public meeting on March 13, 1919. Its membership was sparse, its finances low. Most of the leaders in education at that time gave it but scant attention. It was destined, however, to arouse the enthusiasm of both the school world and the general public to a degree unprecedented in American educational history.

From several points of view, the infant association was fortunate in its early leadership. Main crusader in the creation of the group was Stanwood Cobb, a young instructor in English at the United States Naval Academy. His contributions were those of informed dedication and zeal. Associated with him were Charles W. Eliot, president-emeritus of Harvard, the group's first honorary president, and Arthur E. Morgan, a conservation engineer, its first active president. Still a figure of controversy, Eliot was nonetheless the leading elder statesman of American education, by virtue of both his 85 years and his distinguished career. Morgan, referred to as a great outsider in education, brought to the association the world of affairs beyond the school. Outsider, however, he did not long remain, for he shortly accepted the presidency of Antioch College, becoming thereby a successor of Horace Mann.

The association's membership in this early period consisted largely of teachers in what were known as experimental schools, parents who had children in such schools, and others who wanted to foster pedagogical change. Many of the experimental schools then in existence were private, but public schools were represented as well. Cobb was soon to start a private experimental school at Chevy Chase, Maryland. These schools were by no means alike. The leaders of the group in this early period did not seek uniformity of practice, and Cobb emphasized the dangers of a narrow basis in doctrine.

What they were against was clear, namely, the alleged regimentation, lock-step methods, and suppression of children in schools, particularly those of large public school systems. Frequently disparaged in their utterances were practices referred to under such stereotypes as traditional teaching, meaningless drill, and harsh or repressive discipline. What they were for was less easy to state.

In spite of the diversity represented, the association did manage to produce a platform, the seven points of which were as follows: "Freedom to develop naturally," meaning the freedom of the child; "Interest, the motive of all work," a favorite idea with Eliot; "The teacher a guide, not a taskmaster"; "Scientific study of pupil development"; "Greater attention to all that affects the child's physical development"; "Cooperation between home and school"; and "The progressive school a leader in educational movements."[1] There was no hint of anti-intellectualism, or if there was, it escaped the attention of Eliot, who had devoted his career to mental training as an aim of education.

Obviously the association did not invent the ideas in its platform. They had come from many sources, including in their immediate context the child-study movement of the 1890s. In their 1915 book about experimental schools, entitled *Schools of Tomorrow,* John and Evelyn Dewey said the practices were based on theories that went back as far as Plato.[2] Neither did the association invent the term *progressive education,* although the use of this particular combination of words was infrequent before 1919. The modifier *progressive,* however, had been widely used in education, usually with

[1] Progressive Education Association, *Progressive Education Advances* (New York: D. Appleton-Century Company, 1938), pp. 5–6.
[2] John and Evelyn Dewey, *Schools of Tomorrow* (New York: E. P. Dutton & Company, 1915), unnumbered page in preface.

such substantives as schools, practices, and teaching. Whether it meant what the association believed in would be difficult to determine, especially since the members believed in many things. It is perhaps futile to seek a true definition of progressive education. The ideas involved in it were fluid indeed.

During this early period and throughout the 1920s there were some common themes. Most persistent of these probably were individuality and freedom. In one sense, the association was a protest movement, not only against conventional teaching but also against the stern doctrines of social efficiency and social control being voiced by leading educators at that time.

The advocates of individuality and freedom insisted that they did not mean irresponsibility or license. There was a social aspect to their views as well, thus raising again the perennial dilemma of the individual and the group. Eliot himself had advocated both individual freedom and a strong sense of community obligation. The stress on individuality, however, soon created a public stereotype of a progressive school as one in which disorder reigned supreme.

Noteworthy in the early work of the association was the presence of so-called lay people, that is, those not professionally employed in teaching. This was dramatically exemplified in the Moraine Park School of Dayton, Ohio, an experimental school that had been started in 1917–1918 by ten leading and nonteaching citizens of the community. Among these were Arthur E. Morgan, the association's first president and at that time chief engineer of the Miami Conservation District; Orville Wright, coinventor of the airplane; Fred Rike, president of a department store; and Charles F. Kettering, an executive of the General Motors Research Laboratory. Part of the school was located on Kettering's estate. Tuition was adjusted to the ability of the parents to pay. Financial deficits were largely made up by Kettering and one other industrialist.

Neither progressive education nor the participation of nonteaching citizens was confined to private schools. One of the most widely-known centers of progressive education was the public school system of Winnetka, Illinois, with Carleton W. Washburne as superintendent, and with the active involvement of other community leaders, such as Mrs. Rose Alschuler.

As the 1920s moved along, so-called professional educators increasingly joined and took active part in the association. Whether this affected the ideology of the group would be difficult to determine. Among the most widely known of the professional educators were John Dewey and William Heard Kilpatrick, both of Columbia University. Although he had sponsored one of the earliest experimental schools, that of the University of Chicago (1896–1904), Dewey at the outset did not join the association. In 1924, he succeeded Eliot as honorary president. Because of this and his role as a leading student of educational questions, Dewey was regarded by some as the ideological father of the movement. He did not, however, always agree with what was said or done in his name and at times scolded some of his followers for their presumed misinterpretations of his ideas.

The movement had an international character as well. Especially in England and Germany there were experimental schools with ideals and practices similar to those in the United States. Like those in the United States, many of the European experimental schools predated the association. Whether or not the schools of Russia in this period were examples of progressive education has long been a subject for debate. Whatever such tendencies may have existed, these were sharply repudiated in the 1930s by the Stalin regime.

In this country progressive education by 1930 had become a widespread and familiar term. Practically all teachers and many of their fellow citizens formed strong views on both sides. Membership increased with the impression in some quarters that progressive education held the key to the future. During the 1930s, the ideology of the association shifted somewhat to more concern about social problems and social forces, particularly involving a point of view known as social reconstructionism, one that was widely debated within the group.

It was in the 1930s that the association created its Commission on the Relation of School and College. Aided by grants from the

General Education Board, a philanthropic agency, the commission sponsored what became known popularly as the Eight-Year Study, the first classes under which were started in the fall of 1933. Several hundred leading colleges and universities agreed to accept on the recommendations of principals the graduates of thirty selected secondary schools, without stipulation of patterns of subjects for entrance. The purpose was to free these schools for creative experimentation, and they became known as the thirty unshackled schools. Fifteen of these were public high schools.

To help the schools exercise their freedom, the association also created the Commission on the Secondary-School Curriculum, a consultant group. There was no common pattern of experimentation, but much attention was paid in some schools to the development of core classes. These were classes freed from the aims of the separate subjects; their aims were to meet the common problems and needs of students, in which process subject matter was used. An evaluation staff conducted research. Of greatest interest to the public was the finding that the students from the experimental or unshackled schools did as well in college as those from schools bound by subject requirements. Many concluded from these findings that college admission requirements, in the sense of required subjects, were a thing of the past. If the colleges shared this view, they did not put it into practice.

With the 1940s came a widespread public reaction against so-called progressive education. It was blamed for the presumed inadequacies of American youth in the fundamentals, a concern intensified by the pressures of war. Defenders of progressive education charged these defects, to whatever extent they may have existed, to the widespread persistence of conventional schooling.

As criticism increased, membership declined. In 1944, the name was changed to the American Education Fellowship, followed in 1953 by a return to that of the Progressive Education Association, which had earlier (1920) replaced the original and longer name. Two years later the association disbanded. Whether or not an entity called progressive education survived became in some quarters a favorite topic of discussion. Perhaps the National Science Foundation projects, started in the late 1950s, with their stress upon creative inquiry rather than absorption of content, represented a new version of what had been at least part of the association's point of view.

During its thirty-six years of existence the association functioned as a creative force in American education. Like the Committee of Ten, it was much talked about. Perhaps like that committee, its greatest contribution lay in the questions it stirred up. As late as 1965, nothing like it had arisen to take its place.

Suggestions for Additional Reading

Aikin, Wilford. *The Story of the Eight-Year Study*. New York: Harper & Row, 1942.

Cobb, Stanwood. *New Horizons for the Child*. Washington, D.C.: The Avalon Press, 1934.

Cremin, Lawrence A. *The Transformation of the School*. New York: Alfred A. Knopf, 1961.

Progressive Education Association. *Progressive Education Advances*. New York: D. Appleton-Century Company, 1938. Contains the 1919 platform, pp. 5–6.

Washburne, Carleton W., and Sydney P. Marland, Jr. *Winnetka: The History and Significance of an Educational Experiment*. Englewood Cliffs, N.J.: Prentice-Hall, Inc., 1963.

Meyer v. *Nebraska*

IN A MAJORITY DECISION written by Justice James C. McReynolds, the United States Supreme Court on June 4, 1923, set aside the conviction of a teacher in a private school who had violated a Nebraska law against teaching a foreign language in the elementary grades. Although specifically protecting the rights of individuals to pursue their occupations, the decision in this case, *Meyer* v. *Nebraska,* has been widely interpreted as setting limits to the powers of states in the control of private schools. Beyond this, it raised and dealt with issues pertaining to the use of schools as instruments of public policy.

The law violated by teacher Meyer had been enacted in 1919. Similar to those passed by a number of states at that time, it was a by-product of the campaign for Americanization through the schools. It prohibited the teaching of a foreign language in the first eight grades of any public or private school and also proscribed the teaching of any subject through the medium of a foreign tongue. In the specific case under consideration, Meyer had been engaged in the process of teaching German to a pupil in the elementary grades of the Zion Evangelical Lutheran School of Hamilton County on May 25, 1920, between one o'clock and one-thirty in the afternoon.

Meyer's appeal had gone first to the Supreme Court of Nebraska, where the statute was upheld in a decision filed on February 16, 1922. In this decision, the ideology of the law was made abundantly clear. Its purpose, called "salutary" by the Nebraska court, was that of making the English language "the mother tongue of all the children in the state" and was justified as an application of the state's police power.[1]

"The legislature," continued the Nebraska decision, "had seen the baneful effect of permitting foreigners, who had taken residence in this country, to rear and educate their children in the language of their native land," a condition that had, according to the court, been "found to be inimical to our own safety." With regard to citizens "who are not of foreign ancestry" who might have wanted their children to learn a foreign tongue, the Nebraska court found no serious problem, for these "except in rare instances, have never deemed it of importance to teach their children foreign languages before such children reached the eighth grade." Apparently forgotten were the efforts of the New England Latin Grammar Schools to do this very thing, although the Nebraska court did exempt "the so-called ancient or dead languages."

Eventually the case came before the Supreme Court of the United States, where it was scrutinized in the light of the Fourteenth Amendment's restrictions on the rights of states to deprive persons of life, liberty, or property without due process of law. "Mere knowledge of the German language," wrote Justice McReynolds in the majority decision, "cannot reasonably be regarded as harmful. Heretofore it has been commonly looked upon as helpful and desirable."[2] It seemed, therefore, to the majority of the court that Meyer had a right to teach it in the exercise of his occupation. He was exercising a right of which he should not be deprived. The decision of the Nebraska Supreme Court was reversed.

The decision did not stop with this, but went on to make general observations about the police power of states with respect to schools. It recognized the desire of Nebraska "to promote civic development" by forbidding the teaching of foreign languages to children "before they could learn English and acquire American ideals." Granting that a state may "go very far, indeed, in order to improve the quality

[1] *Robert T. Meyer* v. *State of Nebraska,* 57 Neb. 657 (1922).
[2] *Meyer* v. *Nebraska,* 262 U.S. 390 (1923).

of its citizens," the decision insisted nonetheless that "the individual has certain fundamental rights which must be respected." Advantageous as it might be to promote the use of a common tongue, "this cannot be coerced by methods which conflict with the Constitution —a desirable end cannot be promoted by prohibited means."

Turning to past philosophies and governments, the decision noted that Plato had recommended the common rearing of the young by officers of the state and that Sparta, "in order to submerge the individual and develop ideal citizens," had intrusted the education of males above the age of seven to such official guardians. These ideas, thought the majority of the court, were "wholly different from those upon which our institutions rest."

The decision also clearly stated that it raised no question about "the power of the State to compel attendance at some school and to make reasonable regulations for all schools, including a requirement that they shall give instructions in English." Neither did it challenge "the State's power to prescribe a curriculum for institutions which it supports." Returning again to Meyer's right to pursue his occupation, the decision pointed out that such occupation might be suitably regulated by the state, but that "mere abuse" incidental to its pursuit did not justify its being abolished.

At the very end of the decision, McReynolds indulged himself in the always-popular discussion of child psychology and pedagogy. Since the Nebraska law interfered only with the teaching of a foreign language, it evidently did not, in his opinion and that of the majority of the court, seek to protect the child's health by limiting his mental activities. "It is well known," he observed, that "proficiency in a foreign language seldom comes to one not instructed at an early age, and experience shows that this is not injurious to the health, morals or understanding of the ordinary child."

Included in the report of this case was a dissenting opinion, written by Justice Oliver Wendell Holmes, Jr., and concurred in by Justice George Sutherland. If there were parts of a state where a child would hear only a foreign tongue at home, wrote Holmes, he was "not prepared to say that it is unreasonable to provide that in his early years he shall hear and speak only English at school." If this was not unreasonable, it did not then constitute undue restriction on teachers.

"No one would doubt," Holmes continued, "that a teacher might be forbidden to teach many things, and the only criterion of this liberty under the Constitution that I can think of is 'whether, considering the end in view, the statute passes the bound of reason and assumes the character of a merely arbitrary fiat.' " He felt this had not been true in Nebraska. In a related case, ruled on by the court in the context of the Meyer decision, where the state of Ohio had forbidden only the teaching of German, Holmes agreed with the majority that the restriction was unreasonable.

Suggestion for Additional Reading

McCoy, Raymond F. *American School Administration: Public and Catholic.* New York: McGraw-Hill Book Company, Inc., 1961. Contains the majority decision in *Meyer* v. *Nebraska,* pp. 391–395.

Life Adjustment Education

THE TERM *life adjustment education* was officially unveiled on June 1, 1945, at the end of a two-day conference sponsored by the United States Office of Education on "Vocational Education in the Years Ahead." As often happens in conferences, the participants were not quite sure what they had agreed on, and the chairman called upon one of them, Charles A. Prosser, to summarize the sense of the meeting. Prosser's summary, expressed as a resolution, was accepted by the group. Embedded in it was the new term, destined for a decade to elicit much applause and subsequently to become the scapegoat for the shedding of pedagogical sins.

All this still lay ahead as Prosser began to read his resolution on that June afternoon in 1945. "It is the belief of this conference," he said, "that, with the aid of this report in final form, the vocational school of a community will be able better to prepare 20 percent of its youth of secondary-school age for entrance upon desirable skilled occupations; and that the high school will continue to prepare 20 percent of its students for entrance to college. We do not believe that the remaining 60 percent of our youth of secondary-school age will receive the life adjustment training they need and to which they are entitled as American citizens—unless and until the administrators of public education with the assistance of the vocational education leaders formulate a comparable program for this group."[1] The resolution went on to request the commissioner of

[1] Quoted in Maris M. Proffitt, "Secondary School Life Adjustment Training for Sixty Percent of Our Youth," *School Life*, XXVIII (July, 1946), p. 6.

education to call a conference or a series of regional conferences of general and vocational educators to consider the problem and take steps toward its solution.

Charles A. Prosser was a veteran educator who had taken part in such discussions and debates as far back as 1905. As superintendent of schools in New Albany, Indiana, he had led a statewide study program for teachers on the New Harmony movement of Robert Owen and William Maclure. Subsequently he worked as secretary of the National Society for the Promotion of Industrial Education and as first chairman of the Federal Board for Vocational Education. At the time of his famous resolution, he had served with distinction for nearly three decades as director of the William Hood Dunwoody Institute of Minneapolis, a private vocational school.

Reflected in the resolution was a long-term reassessment of the possibilities of technical vocational training. Vocational educators had come to feel that such training, no less than the kind known as academic, demanded students who were interested in schooling and wanted to profit from it. Just how many students were outside this category—and the 60 percent figure was admittedly symbolic—and what they were like posed questions not easily answered. It was this group, presumably, that was not getting life adjustment through the conventional routes.

Commissioner John Studebaker set in motion a number of meetings that led to a national Life Adjustment Conference in Chicago in May, 1947. From this came the creation of the First National Life Adjustment Commission, with Benjamin Willis, superintendent of schools in Yonkers, New York, as chairman. In recommending this commission, the Chicago conference called for all possible ways to improve the life adjustment education of secondary-school youth, an indication that the movement was shifting its attention to the entire population of the high school.

At its work conference held in Washington, D.C., in October, 1948, the commission tried to put together the limited and the comprehensive definitions of the movement. It defined life adjustment education as designed to equip "all American youth to live democratically with satisfaction to themselves and profit to society as home members, workers, and citizens," but with special concern for those who were less well served in the schools than the college-bound or vocational groups.[2] Life adjustment education, then, was meant for all.

The commission also tried to supply a fuller idea of what life adjustment education was to be. There had been much enthusiasm and many meetings, but often the question raised was, "Just what *is* life adjustment education?" The commission's statement began with ethical and moral living, physical, mental, and emotional health; fundamental skills; and wholesome recreation. This was, of course, a paraphrase of some of the aims stated in *Cardinal Principles of Secondary Education* (see *1918*). The commission went on to stress the importance of personal satisfactions, the need for learning experiences appropriate to the capacities of the students, deferred as well as immediate values, creative achievement as well as adjustment to existing conditions, the dignity of work, and the inherent dignity of human personality. Life adjustment education, said the commission, would have many patterns.

In short, schools were urged to experiment. As the conferences went on, leaders in the movement from time to time contributed examples of what various schools were doing in the name of the cause. Speaking to the February, 1949, convention of the National Association of Secondary-School Principals, Chairman Willis mentioned the common-learnings program in Minneapolis, the reorganization of traditional course work at Maplewood-South Orange, New Jersey, a senior core class at Daniel Webster High School in Tulsa, the family-living program of the Academy of the Presentation in San Francisco, and the expansion of agriculture and homemaking subjects at an unnamed school.

Perhaps this flexibility was an element of strength; it turned out also to be a source of weakness. There was little to go on but a slogan; what may have been concrete, whether desirable or not, in

---

[2] Quoted in *A Look Ahead in Secondary Education* (Washington, D.C.: United States Office of Education Bulletin No. 4, 1954), back of cover page.

the early focus on the 60 percent symbol was dissipated by the scattered aim taken at all youth. Chairman Willis and his commission had an impossible task, even though by 1950 twenty states had appointed life adjustment commissions or committees of their own.

The commission retired from its task in the fall of 1950. Its report, *Vitalizing Secondary Education*, was published the following year. A second commission followed, this one with Paul Collier, chief of the Bureau of Youth Services of the State Department of Education in Connecticut, as chairman. It published its report, *A Look Ahead in Secondary Education*, in 1954.

Possibly the movement had already lost some of its force by 1952, when the first blows against it were struck.[3] These were initially directed against some of the problems listed for consideration in the publications of the Illinois Secondary School Curriculum Study, an enterprise related to the Life Adjustment Education Commission of that state. Among these were such items as social skills through dancing and party stunts, improvement of personal appearance, selection of a family dentist, and boy-girl relationships.

These criticisms may have begun to undermine the general reputation of the movement. They helped in any case to identify life adjustment education with the study of immediate personal-social problems. Ironically, where the leaders of the movement had failed to identify it with anything specific, this was now being accomplished by those who opposed it. This identification spread rapidly through the popular press. To the public, life adjustment education came to mean what many regarded as triviality, soft pedagogy, and the neglect of intellectual aims. It is little wonder that with the announcement of the first Russian space satellite in 1957, the immediate reaction throughout the country was that the United States had fallen behind because of life adjustment education.

Probably no other movement in American pedagogy, not even progressive education in its days of decline, had ever come into such

[3] See Arthur E. Bestor, Jr., " 'Life Adjustment' Education: A Critique," *AAUP Journal*, XXXVIII (Autumn, 1952), 413–441; also his "Anti-Intellectualism in the Schools," *The New Republic*, CXXVIII (January 19, 1953), 11–13.

widespread disrepute. Whether or not this was deserved must be left for the calmer judgment of the future. Since the movement itself was vague, it would be difficult to decide what it might be blamed for, perhaps only for the vagueness itself.

Yet the initial question of the Prosser resolution could not be put down. Even in the midst of the so-called academic revival of the late 1950s and early 1960s there continued to be much concern about dropouts and potential dropouts, about those youths who seemed to have no enthusiasms the high schools could arouse.

In February, 1962, Daniel Schreiber, director of the NEA Project on School Dropouts, talked on this point before the convention of the National Association of Secondary-School Principals. He said that the curriculum for the college-bound student, constituting one third of the high-school population, seemed to be good. Another third, he observed, completed the work of business, vocational, or technical schools. The last third, the dropouts, were the problem, and he asked whether it was possible that the curriculum did not hold the interests and satisfy the needs of this group. Although he did not suggest life adjustment education as the solution, his question represented a full swing of the circle back to the Prosser resolution of two decades before.

Suggestions for Additional Reading

Commission on Life Adjustment Education. *Vitalizing Secondary Education*. Washington, D.C.: United States Office of Education Bulletin No. 3, 1951.

Second Commission on Life Adjustment Education for Youth. *A Look Ahead in Secondary Education*. Washington, D.C.: United States Office of Education Bulletin No. 4, 1954.

Brown et al. v. Board of Education of Topeka et al.

RACIAL SEGREGATION BY SCHOOLS, declared the United States Supreme Court on May 17, 1954, deprived the individual of equal protection of the laws, one of the rights guaranteed by the Fourteenth Amendment. In this case, *Brown et al. v. Board of Education of Topeka et al.*, appeals from four states were involved, all of them brought by Negro children, whose contention it was that segregated schools were not equal and could not be made so.

Previous rulings on these cases, three of them by lower federal courts and one by the Supreme Court of Delaware, had upheld the principle of segregation. In so doing, they used what was known as the separate-but-equal doctrine, one that went back to a decision rendered by the United States Supreme Court in *Plessy v. Ferguson* (1896). The court on that occasion had upheld a law of the state of Louisiana providing for equal but separate accommodations on railroad trains.

The question before them, felt the members of the Supreme Court in 1954, could not be resolved merely on whether or not the segregated schools were equal in such "tangible factors" as buildings, curricula, and the qualifications and salaries of teachers. "We must look instead," the court observed, "to the effect of segregation itself on public education." With this the court turned to a discussion of the nature of public education, for "only in this way can it be determined if segregation in public schools deprives these plaintiffs of the equal protection of the laws."[1]

In its pursuit of this point, the court decided that education was probably the most important function of state and local governments, that it was the foundation of citizenship, and that it was "a principal instrument in awakening the child to cultural values, in preparing him for later professional training, and in helping him to adjust normally to his environment." Therefore the opportunity for education, when provided, must be provided to all on equal terms.

Segregated schools, continued the court, had the effect of generating in Negro children "a feeling of inferiority as to their status in the community that may affect their hearts and minds in a way unlikely ever to be undone." It quoted a statement from the United States District Court of Kansas, the one that had nonetheless upheld the validity of separate schools in Topeka, that "a sense of inferiorty affects the motivation of a child to learn" and that segregation sanctioned by law had a tendency to retard the educational and mental development of Negro children.

With this, the court drove with hammerlike sentences to its conclusion: "Whatever may have been the extent of psychological knowledge at the time of *Plessy* v. *Ferguson,* this finding [as quoted from the Kansas court] is amply supported by modern authority. Any language in *Plessy* v. *Ferguson* contrary to this finding is rejected. We conclude that in the field of public education the doctrine of 'separate but equal' has no place. Separate educational facilities are inherently unequal." Such inherent inequality deprived Negro children of the equal protection of the laws.

Critics of the decision have argued that the court went far afield in its use of arguments from psychology and educational history. Its defenders have said that courts on some occasions must draw on

[1] *Brown et al.* v. *Board of Education of Topeka et al.,* 347 U.S. 483 (1954).

resources beyond the narrow channels of the law. Inevitably on broad public questions courts are forced into substantive discussions. These are matters on which judges, as well as others, may disagree. In the Nebraska decision (see *1923*), the majority of the United States Supreme Court believed that it was unreasonable to forbid the teaching of foreign languages in private elementary schools; two of the judges thought otherwise.

The one member of the Supreme Court who had dissented from the majority opinion in the case of *Plessy* v. *Ferguson* in 1896 did so not on the grounds that separate facilities were inherently unequal, but rather on those involving the fundamental justice or injustice of segregation itself. In the eye of the law, wrote Justice Harlin on that occasion, "there is in this country no superior, dominant, ruling class of citizens. There is no caste here. Our Constitution is color-blind, and neither knows nor tolerates classes among citizens. In respect of civil rights, all citizens are equal before the law. . . . It is, therefore, to be regretted that this high tribunal, the final expositor of the fundamental law of the land, has reached the conclusion that it is competent for a State to regulate the enjoyment by citizens of their civil rights solely upon the basis of race."[2]

The 1954 decision was accepted and followed in some states, resisted in others. What it had specifically ruled out, moreover, was *de jure* segregation, that is, segregation as deliberate policy established by law. Much discussion followed about *de facto* segregation, one kind of which reflected the location of boundaries for attendance areas, whether intentional or not. In *Taylor* v. *Board of Education in New Rochelle, New York* (1961), a federal district court ruled against the attendance lines drawn by the school board.

Antisegregationists moved increasingly to the wiping out of *de facto* segregation. This led to numerous controversies in metropolitan communities in the North. Various solutions were proposed and tried, including the widely-debated practice of transporting children in city school systems to schools outside their neighborhoods.

[2] *Plessy* v. *Ferguson,* 163 U.S. 537 (1896).

Suggestions for Additional Reading

Blaustein, A. P., and Clyde C. Ferguson, Jr. *Desegregation and the Law.* New York: Vintage Books, 1962.

Fellman, David (ed.). *The Supreme Court and Education.* (Classics in Education No. 4.) New York: Bureau of Publications, Teachers College, Columbia University, 1962. Contains the 1954 decision, pp. 85–90.

Klopf, G. J., and I. A. Laster. *Integrating the Urban School.* New York: Bureau of Publications, Teachers College, Columbia University, 1963.

"Toward Integration of Northern Schools," *Journal of Educational Sociology,* XXXVI (February, 1963).

★ ★ ★ ★ ★ 1958 ★ ★ ★ ★ ★

The National Defense Education Act (with the Amendments of 1964)

WITH THE APPEARANCE of the Russian space satellite in the fall of 1957 came several sharp reactions throughout American public life, some of them affecting the schools. Among these was the demolition of the image of life adjustment education. Another was the enactment on September 2, 1958, of the National Defense Education Act (hereafter referred to as the NDEA).

The keynote of the NDEA was struck in its opening paragraph: "The Congress hereby finds and declares that the security of the Nation requires the fullest development of the mental resources and technical skills of its young men and women. The present emergency demands that additional and more adequate educational opportunities be made available. The defense of this Nation depends upon the mastery of modern techniques developed from complex scientific principles."[1] Called for by the act was the rapid correction of "existing imbalances in our educational programs which have led to an insufficient proportion of our population educated in science, mathematics, and modern foreign languages and trained in technology."

A major feature of the act was the provision of loans to stu-

[1] National Defense Education Act of 1958, Public Law 85–8642, 85th Congress, September 2, 1958.

dents. Special consideration was recommended for those with superior academic backgrounds who intended to become teachers in elementary or secondary schools and for those whose academic background indicated "a superior capacity or preparation in science, mathematics, engineering, or a modern foreign language." Those who became teachers would have parts of their indebtedness cancelled. Beyond these provisions for loans, there were fellowships for graduate students in new and expanded programs.

Most of the act, however, dealt with financial aids to the states and their subdivisions as sponsors of educational programs. Included were the strengthening of science, mathematics, and foreign languages through the purchase of equipment and materials and the remodeling of space; the establishment and maintenance of programs of testing and counseling and of counseling and guidance training institutes; centers and institutes in foreign languages; research in the use of television, radio, motion pictures, and related media; and the extension of vocational education to residents of areas inadequately served. In some of the foregoing programs, the funds granted by the federal government were to be matched by the states.

Although welcoming support for education, school people and other citizens had mixed feelings about some aspects of NDEA. The act contained a specific disclaimer of federal control, but the granting of funds for some purposes and not for others, known as categorical aid, was feared as a possible influence on the shape of local school programs. Mathematics, for example, was encouraged by federal financial aids, but the fine arts were not. It should be noted, however, that the fellowships for graduate students were not restricted by subjects as such.

Many educators had long favored general federal aid to the states, and a number of such bills had been unsuccessfully introduced in Congress in the past. Such general aid, it was contended, would leave states and local communities free to use the funds for whatever instructional purposes they saw fit. At least, felt some educators, the scope of categorical aids, if continued, should be broadened to include more of the subjects known as humanities and social studies.

Unsuccessful attempts were made in the eighty-seventh Congress, that of 1961–1962, to include such broader provisions in the renewal of the NDEA. The act was again renewed on December 18, 1863, still with the same categories. On October 16, 1964, however, this renewal or extension was substantially modified by amendments that greatly enlarged the scope of the categorical aids.

Stricken out of the opening paragraph in the 1964 amendments was the statement, "which have led to an insufficient proportion of our population educated in science, mathematics, and modern foreign languages and trained in technology." Also deleted was the reference in the section on student loans to special consideration for those planning to teach and those with superior capacity in mathematics, science, engineering, or foreign language.

It was, however, not only the deletions, but the additions that created a new image of NDEA. The list of subjects eligible for aid in the purchase of equipment and materials now included "science, mathematics, history, civics, geography, modern foreign language, English, or reading in public elementary or secondary schools, or both."[2] Beyond the institutes provided in the original act for guidance and modern foreign languages, the amendments added those in history, geography, and reading or English. Another new feature was that of institutes for those "who are engaged in or preparing to engage in the teaching of disadvantaged youth and are, by virtue of their services or future service enrolling substantial numbers of culturally, economically, socially and educationally handicapped youth."

The Elementary and Secondary Education Act approved on April 11, 1965, included a provision of $100,000,000 for the purchase of instructional materials without stipulation as to subjects, thereby broadening the spirit and the scope of the NDEA amendments of the preceding year.

[2] An Act to Amend and Extend the National Defense Act of 1958, Public Law 88–665, 88th Congress, October 16, 1964.

Suggestions for Additional Reading

Burkhead, Jesse. *Public School Finance: Economics and Politics,* with chapters by Bertram M. Gross and Charles S. Benson. Syracuse, N.Y.: Syracuse University Press, 1964. Chaps. X–XIII.

McCoy, Raymond F. *American School Administration: Public and Catholic.* New York: McGraw-Hill Book Company, Inc., 1961. Contains the NDEA of 1958, pp. 421–452.

Sufrin, Sidney C. *Administering the National Defense Education Act.* Syracuse, N.Y.: Syracuse University Press, 1963.

★ ★ ★ ★ ★ **1963** ★ ★ ★ ★ ★

School District of Abington Township, Pennsylvania, et al. v. Schempp et al.

EDUCATION AND RELIGION have always been controversial and exciting subjects. When they come together, the mixture is sensitive and explosive indeed. It is a complex mixture, presenting questions not easy to resolve. Honest differences of opinion arise, and sometimes they come before the courts. So it was on July 17, 1963, when the United States Supreme Court, in *School District of Abington Township, Pennsylvania, et al.* v. *Schempp et al.*, ruled that prayers and Bible exercises in public schools and the laws requiring them were unconstitutional "under the Establishment Clause, as applied to the States through the Fourteenth Amendment."[1]

The Establishment Clause referred to occurs as follows in the First Amendment to the Constitution of the United States: "Congress shall make no law respecting an establishment of religion, or prohibiting the free exercise thereof." Ratified in 1791 as one of the ten amendments constituting the Bill of Rights, the First Amendment was intended to restrict not the states, but the national Congress. The Fourteenth Amendment, ratified in 1868, stated among

---

[1] *School District of Abington Township, Pennsylvania, et al.* v. *Schempp et al.*, 374 U.S. 203 (1963).

other things that "no state shall make or enforce any law which shall abridge the privileges or immunities of citizens of the United States." Under this, the federal courts have applied the Establishment Clause and the provision for free exercise of religion to the states as well.

Until 1868, then, there was nothing to prevent states from having established churches or interfering with freedom of religion unless they chose so to restrict themselves through their own constitutions and laws. A state could make laws requiring public schools to hold religious exercises. Even after 1868, there was for many years little explicit or practical awareness of the impact of the Fourteenth Amendment on the First. The result was that state constitutions and laws provided a confusing medley of practices that were in some cases prohibited, in some permitted, and in some required in public schools.

Inevitably, disputes on such matters came to the federal judicial system. Particularly open to controversy was the meaning of the Establishment Clause. Much discussion took place on what the founding fathers had meant by it. Special attention was centered on what Jefferson had thought it meant, for although not present at the Constitutional Convention he had taken much part in discussions of religious freedom. In a letter to a committee of the Danbury Baptist Association, Connecticut, dated January 1, 1802, Jefferson said that the First Amendment had built a wall of separation between church and state, an expression that was to occur frequently in the decisions of the courts.

The ruling on the Schempp case in 1963 had been preceded by a number of cases involving religion, education, and the state. Not all of these had dealt with religious practices in public schools; neither did they all invoke the Establishment Clause.

In *Cochran* v. *Louisiana State Board of Education* (1930), the court had upheld the right of the state to supply textbooks to children in private, including parochial, schools. Here the complainants had invoked section 4 of Article IV of the Constitution, guaranteeing to each state a republican form of government. In *Everson* v. *Board of Education* (1947), the court upheld a New Jersey law under which children in parochial schools were transported in the regular school buses. Although this case did not involve religious practices, it brought up a long examination by the court of the meaning of the Establishment Clause. The court decided here that the wall of separation between church and state had not been breached.

Two cases dealing with provisions in public schools for released time for religious instruction conducted by churches brought matters closer to the issue of religious practices. In one of these, *Illinois ex re McCollum* v. *Board of Education* (1948), the court invoked the Establishment Clause to rule against the released-time provisions. In the second case, *Zorach* v. *Clauson* (1952), the court upheld a released-time provision in the New York City schools. The difference, according to the majority of the court, lay in the fact that the classes in New York City were not held on the school premises.

With *Engel* v. *Vitale* (1962), the court moved specifically to religious exercises in classrooms. Here the point at issue was the use of a prayer adopted under the auspices of the New York State Board of Regents and recommended by them to the local schools. The court invalidated the use of this prayer as a violation of the Establishment Clause, directing attention to the fact that the prayer had been composed officially by an agency of the state.

Controversy followed as to whether or not this decision ruled out other kinds of religious exercises in public schools, particularly if these were not composed by official bodies. Specifically involved in the Schempp decision of 1963 was a state law of Pennsylvania that required the reading without comment of ten verses from the Bible at the opening of each school day in public schools. Provision was made in the law for excusing children from this on written request from parents. The practice in the Abington Senior High School was to broadcast the Bible reading over the intercommunication system to the home rooms between 8:15 and 8:30 in the morning.

In the companion case ruled on at the same time, suit had been brought against the Board of School Commissioners of Baltimore with respect to a local rule that called for opening exercises with Bible reading or the use of the Lord's Prayer or both. The local rule was authorized under the state law. Although the board amended the rule to provide for the excusing of pupils on parental request, the petitioners contended that it still violated freedom of religion and the separation of church and state.

The Schempp decision was a long one, involving much historical and philosophical discourse and many references to previous cases. In addition to the statement of the majority decision, there were three concurring opinions and one in dissent. In summary, the majority opinion held that the practices under consideration in Pennsylvania and in Baltimore were religious ceremonies and as such out of place in public schools.

Since the court ruled out not only the laws requiring these practices, but also the practices themselves, it presumably forbade any prayers or Bible readings in public schools. There remained, however, the possibility of cases in which state laws or rules of local school boards did not form part of the context. The other possibility left open to those who advocated such readings and prayers was to amend the Constitution of the United States. A movement was launched in this direction, but by the end of 1964 it had not been approved in Congress.

In any event, there was little likelihood that the Schempp decision would close the debate. There were those who agreed with the dissenting opinion of Justice Stewart that the practices involved did not constitute a violation of the Establishment Clause. The question remained one of substantive definition, with speeches delivered from many points of view. The issue was not drawn as such between church people and those opposed to churches. Most of the opponents of religious practices in public schools disclaimed any feeling of hostility toward religion. Some religious denominations were themselves among the most strenuous advocates of separation between church and state.

Suggestions for Additional Reading

Duker, Sam. *Religion and the Public Schools.* New York: Harper & Row, 1965. Contains extensive portions of the Schempp decision along with other decisions on religion and public schools.

Fellman, David (ed.). *The Supreme Court and Education.* (Classics in Education No. 4.) New York: Bureau of Publications, Teachers College, Columbia University, 1962. Contains the Cochran and Everson cases, pp. 5–30, and the McCollum, Zorach, and Engle cases, pp. 45–76.

Leading Decisions of the United States Supreme Court. (Individually bound.) San Francisco: Chandler Publishing Company, undated series. Includes individual pamphlet reprints of the Schempp, Everson, and McCollum cases.

The Economic Opportunity Act

ALTHOUGH THE CONSTITUTION said nothing about schools, national policy in the United States on many occasions has included the development and use of educational resources. So it was in the Northwest Ordinance (see *1787*), an instrument that predated the Constitution itself. It was with the broad national interest in view that Congress enacted the Land Grant College Act (see *1862*), the Smith-Hughes and other acts pertaining to vocational education (see *1917*), and the National Defense Education Act (see *1958*), with its 1964 amendments. In all probability, however, no preceding legislation wove education into the national effort to the degree represented by the Economic Opportunity Act, signed by President Lyndon B. Johnson on August 20, 1964.

This was a war against poverty. By 1964 it had become painfully clear that in the midst of unprecedented national prosperity there were millions of American citizens with incomes below the minimal standards for health, the enjoyment of living, and the providing of opportunities to their children.

"It is, therefore," declared the preamble to the Economic Opportunity Act of 1964, "the policy of the United States to eliminate the paradox of poverty in the midst of plenty in this Nation by opening to everyone the opportunity for education and training, the opportunity to work, and the opportunity to live in decency and dignity."[1] The Act was more than an enterprise in which education

[1] Economic Opportunity Act of 1964, Public Law 88–452, 88th Congress, August 20, 1964.

would be called upon to take part. It was in itself a national enterprise in education.

Such legislation as this was necessarily complex, and the act had many parts. Included in it were youth programs, urban and rural community action programs, special programs to combat poverty in rural areas, employment and investment incentives, and work experience programs for unemployed fathers and other needy persons.

The major feature of the youth programs was the Job Corps, including provisions for conservation camps and for training centers. Enrollees in the conservation camps were youths who had not finished high school and who had not found satisfactory employment. In addition to their pay, the enrollees were provided with full living expenses, including medical and recreational services, during their period of study and work. Each camp was to number about 200 enrollees, with staff members including a deputy for education, a guidance counselor, and teachers for reading, arithmetic, science, and citizenship. The first camps, similar in some respects to those of the Civilian Conservation Corps of thirty years before, were opened early in 1965.

The training centers, also part of the Job Corps, were located near large cities and directed more specifically to vocational education. Programs similar to those in the conservation camps and the training centers were provided for women, but in smaller residential units and including education for family life.

Also included in the broad program for youth were work-training programs for unemployed youth from low-income families. These provided not only work with pay on public projects and those of private nonprofit organizations, but also work experience and training in occupational skills. Accompanying these were work-study programs to aid youth who were students in institutions of higher education.

There were also programs for adults. Since illiteracy in adults often becomes a handicap in employment, provision was made under a basic-education program for teaching those over eighteen years of age to read and write. Further opportunities for adults under the act were offered in the form of loans to those engaged in small business concerns. As a condition for these loans, the recipients might be required to take part in management-training programs.

The educational nature of the act was evident not only in the foregoing provisions, but also in those portions calling for community action programs. These involved the participations of citizens in the study and solution of problems of poverty in their local areas. The term *community action programs* was defined in the act as activities which mobilized many kinds of resources in direct attack on the causes of poverty and which would be "developed, conducted, and administered with the maximum feasible participation of residents of the areas and members of the groups served."

Implied in the act and made explicit by the director in its early stages was a call for participation by formal agencies of education. Superintendents of schools were asked through the American Association of School Administrators to grant leaves of absence to teachers willing to serve in the Job Corps. It was hoped that such teachers would return to their schools not only with the satisfaction of having made an important contribution, but also with valuable experience in the teaching of culturally-deprived youth.

Additional provision for the use of education as a weapon against poverty was made in the Elementary and Secondary Education Act of 1965. In Title I, of this act, Congress stipulated $1,060,082,973 to be apportioned for general school purposes to local systems on the basis of the number of school children in families with incomes of less than $2000 a year. The act also provided funds to states for the purchase and distribution of instructional materials, the creation of supplementary education centers, and the strengthening of their departments of education. National and regional agencies were given funds for the carrying on of educational research.

The Economic Opportunity Act of 1964 was a new kind of venture, but it combined many features of the American pedagogical tradition. Although it did not make direct subsidies to gifted youth or propose that the benefits be limited to the topmost few, the work-study program reflected Jefferson's conviction that youth of promise should not be denied higher education because of lack of money. It reflected Horace Mann's belief that social and economic problems could be solved by orderly and peaceful means. Education, he had written in his *Twelfth Annual Report* in 1848, prevented being poor. These sentiments have at times been greeted with skepticism, amusement, pessimism, even hostility. Always sustaining these sentiments has been yet another element in the American tradition, a supreme degree of optimism as to what education could accomplish. In the Economic Opportunity Act of 1964 was faith that education could remove one of the oldest and most grievous ills of mankind.

Suggestions for Additional Reading

Drennan, Henry T. (ed.). "The War on Poverty," *Library Journal,* LXXXIX (September 15, 1964), 3239–3273 and 3376–3389. Various articles on the Economic Opportunity Act.

"Education and Poverty," *Saturday Review,* XLVIII (May 15, 1965), 68–74, 85–89.

Harrington, Michael. *The Other America: Poverty in the United States.* New York: The Macmillan Company, 1962.

"Poverty and the School," *Educational Leadership,* XXII (May, 1965). Entire issue.

Index